FROM THE KITCHENS OF

HEALTHY*CHOICE®

FOODS

OVEN-ROASTED Etc.

MEALS FOR LIFE™

CY DeCOSSE
INCORPORATED

A COWLES MAGAZINES COMPANY

CY DECOSSE INCORPORATED
A COWLES MAGAZINES COMPANY

Chairman/CEO: Bruce Barnet
Chairman Emeritus: Cy DeCosse
President/COO: Nino Tarantino
Executive V.P./Editor-in-Chief:
  William B. Jones

Healthy Choice© is a registered trademark of ConAgra Inc.
used under license by Cy DeCosse Incorporated.

Printed on American paper by:
Quebecor Graphics (0196)
Copyright © 1996
Cy DeCosse Incorporated
5900 Green Oak Drive
Minnetonka, Minnesota 55343
1-800-328-3895
All rights reserved
Printed in U.S.A.

Library of Congress Cataloging-in-Publication Data

Oven-roasted etc.
p. cm. -- (Meals for life™)
Includes index.
ISBN 0-86573-978-1
1. Convection oven cookery.   I. Cy DeCosse Incorporated.
II. Series.
TX840.C65094 1996
641.5'8--dc20   95-41893

Table of Contents

*O*ven-roasted Etc. gives you recipes for more relaxed meal preparation. Oven-cooked recipes usually take a little while to get done, but that extra time lets you prepare the other parts of the meal without feeling rushed.

The *Etc.* in the title means that you'll find recipes for a variety of oven-cooking techniques, including roasting, baking, casserole cooking and oven frying. In addition, we've included recipes that utilize other cooking techniques, so you can prepare them ahead of time or while your main dish is in the oven. Traditional baked goods, like breads and cakes, are not included in this book.

Menu suggestions appear with every recipe to aid in meal planning. These suggestions include recipes from this book as well as simple complementary dishes. They are selected with easy meal planning in mind.

Menu suggestions focus only on the main components of the meal. Beverages and dessert ideas are not included. Balance the menus with fresh fruit and vegetables, low-fat milk, and breads. Choose low-fat refreshing desserts, like fruit or sorbet, that won't fill you up or out.

Equipment

Baking pans, made of metal, can be round, square, rectangular of loaf-shaped. Baking dishes come in the same shapes and sizes but are made of glass or ceramic. Dishes can be substituted for pans, but you will have to decrease the oven temperature by 25°F to prevent over-browning.

There are no standard sizes for baking pans and dishes. We've shown a few of the more common sizes here, but there are many others that can be used. When measuring, measure from inside edge to inside edge. If using a larger pan than called for, decrease the baking time slightly. If using a smaller pan, increase the baking time and watch for overflow.

(1) 9-inch deep-dish pie plate; **(2)** 12 x 8-inch baking dish; **(3)** 8-inch square baking dish; **(4)** 2-quart round casserole; **(5)** baking sheet without edges; **(6)** baking sheet with edges; **(7)** 13 x 9-inch baking pan; **(8)** roasting pan with rack; **(9)** broiler pan with rack; **(10)** 8-inch square baking pan; **(11)** 9 x 5-inch loaf pan

Roasting & Baking

Roasting is a dry-heat cooking technique for preparing larger cuts of meat and poultry, and vegetables such as corn, potatoes and peppers. Food is cooked uncovered with all sides exposed to the heat. This method produces a browned, crusty exterior and a juicy interior. It is a fairly gentle cooking technique, but, occasionally, marinating foods before roasting, or basting them while roasting, is necessary to keep them from drying out. This is especially true of very lean cuts of meat.

Baking differs from roasting in that it is used for ham, fish and smaller cuts of meat and poultry. Food may be cooked uncovered or covered and is in a pan that has higher sides to prevent all sides of the food from being directly exposed to heat.

For large roasts, you will want to use a meat thermometer to judge doneness (see photos at right). Use an instant-read thermometer for small cuts and pieces, but do not leave it in the oven. Most instant-read thermometers are not ovenproof.

Using a Meat Thermometer

Measure the distance from the outside of the roast to the center of the thickest muscle. With your fingers, mark the point where the thermometer touches the edge of the meat.

Insert thermometer to depth marked by your fingers. The tip should be in center of meat, not touching fat or bone. With a flat roast, insert the thermometer into the end so at least 2 inches of the stem is in the meat.

Casseroles

Casseroles are one of the most convenient dishes to prepare. They can be cooked and served in the same dish, and often consist of a mixture of ingredients that constitute a one-dish meal. They are easy to make, can be prepared ahead of time and freeze well. Casserole is also the name of the dish in which these recipes are prepared.

Oven Frying

Oven frying is a technique that gives foods the flavor and appearance of traditionally fried foods, but with much less fat. Foods like fish, chicken or veal scallops are usually brushed with margarine or butter, or are dipped in yogurt, milk or beaten egg whites, and then coated with seasoned flour or a crumb mixture. Then they are baked on a baking sheet until they are browned.

7

10

11

9

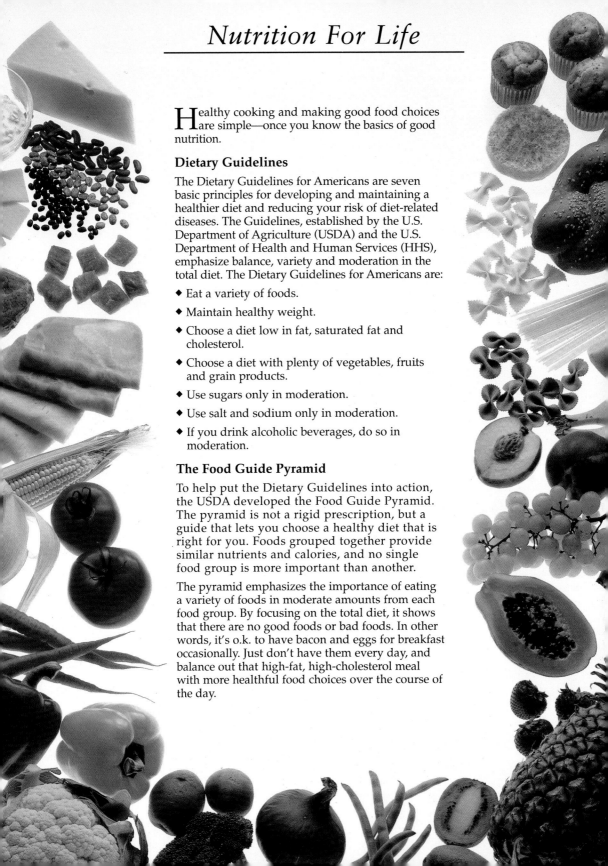

Nutrition For Life

Healthy cooking and making good food choices are simple—once you know the basics of good nutrition.

Dietary Guidelines

The Dietary Guidelines for Americans are seven basic principles for developing and maintaining a healthier diet and reducing your risk of diet-related diseases. The Guidelines, established by the U.S. Department of Agriculture (USDA) and the U.S. Department of Health and Human Services (HHS), emphasize balance, variety and moderation in the total diet. The Dietary Guidelines for Americans are:

- Eat a variety of foods.
- Maintain healthy weight.
- Choose a diet low in fat, saturated fat and cholesterol.
- Choose a diet with plenty of vegetables, fruits and grain products.
- Use sugars only in moderation.
- Use salt and sodium only in moderation.
- If you drink alcoholic beverages, do so in moderation.

The Food Guide Pyramid

To help put the Dietary Guidelines into action, the USDA developed the Food Guide Pyramid. The pyramid is not a rigid prescription, but a guide that lets you choose a healthy diet that is right for you. Foods grouped together provide similar nutrients and calories, and no single food group is more important than another.

The pyramid emphasizes the importance of eating a variety of foods in moderate amounts from each food group. By focusing on the total diet, it shows that there are no good foods or bad foods. In other words, it's o.k. to have bacon and eggs for breakfast occasionally. Just don't have them every day, and balance out that high-fat, high-cholesterol meal with more healthful food choices over the course of the day.

The Food Guide Pyramid

Fats, Oils & Sweets
Use sparingly

**Milk, Yogurt &
Cheese Group**
2-3 Servings per day

**Meat, Poultry, Fish, Dry
Beans, Eggs & Nuts Group**
2-3 Servings per day

Vegetable Group
3-5 Servings per day

Fruit Group
2-4 Servings per day

**Bread, Cereal, Rice
& Pasta Group**
6-11 Servings
per day

Reading the Pyramid

It's easy to follow the Food Guide Pyramid.

The bottom of the pyramid shows complex carbohydrates—the bread, cereal, rice and pasta group—at 6-11 servings a day. This group should be the foundation of a healthy diet.

The second level is made up of fruits and vegetables. We need to eat 3-5 servings of vegetables and 2-4 servings of fruit each day.

The third level is divided equally between milk, yogurt and cheese (2-3 servings a day) and meat, poultry, fish, beans, eggs and nuts (2-3 servings a day).

Most supermarkets now carry skim or low-fat milk and buttermilk; low-fat or nonfat yogurt, cottage cheese or ricotta cheese; and other low-fat cheeses.

A large variety of lean cuts of meat is also available in most stores. The leanest cuts of beef are the round, loin, sirloin and chuck arm. Pork tenderloin, center loin or lean ham, and all cuts of veal, except ground veal, are relatively lean. For lamb, the leanest cuts are the leg, loin and foreshanks. Chicken and turkey with the skin removed and most fish are lean meat choices.

The tip of the pyramid shows fats, oils and sweets. These include foods such as salad dressings, cream, butter, margarine, sugars, soft drinks and candies. Use them sparingly.

Build a diet of good food choices based on complex carbohydrates, and limit your intake of high-fat foods. The recipes in this book make it easy to fit nutritious meals into a busy schedule. And you don't have to choose between good taste and good nutrition. You can have them both.

Balancing Your Diet

The number of servings per day that is right for you depends on the amount of calories you need to maintain your best weight. The USDA recommends the following calorie levels per day: 1600 calories for many sedentary women and some older adults; 2200 calories for most children, teenage girls, active women and many sedentary men; and 2800 calories for teenage boys, many active men and some very active women. Each person's body is different, however, and you may need more or less depending on your age, sex, size, activity level and medical condition.

For example, if your calorie intake level is in the lower range, choose the smaller number of servings in each food group. Or, if you are very active, choose the larger number of servings in each group.

Serving Sizes

What counts as a serving?

You may be surprised. Use this chart to determine how your food intake compares to servings on the pyramid.

For combination foods, use your best judgment in estimating which food groups they fall into. For example, a large serving of pasta with tomato sauce and cheese could count in the bread group, the vegetable group and the milk group.

Milk, Yogurt & Cheese Group

2 ounces processed cheese, preferably reduced fat

1 cup low-fat milk or yogurt

1½ ounces natural cheese, preferably reduced fat

Meat, Poultry & Fish Group

½ cup cooked dry beans, 1 egg or 2 tablespoons peanut butter count as 1 ounce lean meat

2-3 ounces cooked lean meat, poultry or fish

Vegetable Group

1 cup raw leafy vegetables

½ cup other vegetables, cooked or raw

¾ cup vegetable juice

Fruit Group

¾ cup fruit juice

½ cup chopped, cooked or canned fruit

1 medium apple, banana or orange

Bread, Cereal, Rice & Pasta Group

1 muffin, dinner roll or slice bread

1 ounce ready-to-eat cereal

½ cup cooked cereal, rice or pasta

2 Add juice, wine, sugar, salt, marjoram and pepper to skillet. Cover. Reduce heat to low. Let simmer for 12 to 15 minutes, or until meat near bone is no longer pink and juices run clear.

3 Remove chicken from skillet and place on serving platter. Cover to keep warm. Set aside. Using whisk, stir cornstarch mixture into skillet. Add grapes and peel. Cook for 1½ to 2½ minutes, or until sauce is thickened and translucent, stirring constantly. Spoon over chicken.

Nutrition Facts	Amount/serving	%DV*	Amount/serving	%DV*
Serving Size 1 breast half (136g)	Total Fat 5g	7%	Total Carbohydrate 9g	3%
	Saturated Fat 1g	5%	Dietary Fiber <1g	1%
Servings per Recipe 6	Cholesterol 55mg	18%	Sugars 8g	
Calories 164 Calories from Fat 41	Sodium 135mg	6%	Protein 21g	
	Vitamin A 0% • Vitamin C 20% • Calcium 2% • Iron 4%			
	*Percent Daily Values (DV) are based on a 2000 calorie diet			

Menu Planning Guide
One serving of this recipe provides
1 Meat, Poultry & Fish
½ Fruit

Diet Exchanges:
3 lean meat • ½ fruit

Nutritional Information

Each recipe in this book is followed by a Nutrition Facts chart and diet exchanges. The Nutrition Facts chart is similar to those that appear on food product labels. The diet exchange system is used by people with diabetes and persons on a weight-control diet, to estimate the calories, protein, carbohydrate and fat content of a food or meal. Diet exchanges are based on exchange lists and are not the same as pyramid servings.

Nutrition Facts state serving size, servings per container and the amount of calories, calories from fat and other nutrients per serving. Percentage of Daily Value gives you an idea of what percentage of the day's nutrients comes from the recipe. The percentages of the Daily Value of fat, saturated fat, cholesterol, sodium, total carbohydrate and dietary fiber are based on a 2,000-calorie-per-day diet. (Daily values will vary from person to person depending on calorie needs.) The Dietary Guidelines recommend that no more than 30% of your calories come from fat. So, if you are eating 2,000 calories per day, your total fat intake should be less than 65 grams.

If alternate ingredients are given in the recipe's ingredient list, such as a choice between cholesterol-free egg product and egg, the nutritional analysis applies to the first ingredient listed. Optional ingredients are not included in the analysis. For pasta and rice, the nutritional information applies to the plain, boiled item without salt or fat added.

Recipe serving sizes are based on federal reference numbers for serving sizes.

The Pyramid in This Book

Each recipe in this book includes a Menu Planning Guide that shows the number of servings from each pyramid group that one serving of that recipe provides. A daily total of these "pyramid servings" shows how your diet compares to the USDA recommendations.

When the tip of the pyramid has a dot, the item may contain added fat or fat beyond the natural fat content of lean or low-fat items in the food groups. Refer to the Nutrition Facts chart to check the total amount of fat per serving. A tip with a dot may also indicate that the recipe contains added sugar. Refer to the recipe to determine the number of teaspoons of sugar you will eat.

The number of servings is rounded to the nearest half. If no figures appear next to or within the pyramid, it means that serving sizes are negligible.

If the tip of the pyramid has no dot, a serving contains less than 3 grams added fat or less than 1 teaspoon added sugar.

Apple-Sage Stuffed Pork Loin Roast

Serve with steamed asparagus spears and wild rice or Garlic Mashed Potatoes (p 79)

1/4 cup apple jelly

1 tablespoon packed brown sugar

1½ teaspoons Dijon mustard

1 medium red cooking apple, cored and chopped (1 cup)

1 stalk celery, chopped (½ cup)

1 small onion, chopped (½ cup)

2 tablespoons vegetable oil

½ cup unseasoned dry bread crumbs

1/4 cup snipped fresh parsley

2 tablespoons snipped fresh sage leaves

3-lb. well-trimmed boneless pork double loin roast

12 servings

1 Combine jelly, sugar and mustard in 1-quart saucepan. Cook over medium-low heat for 3½ to 5 minutes, or until jelly is melted, stirring constantly. Remove from heat. Set glaze aside.

2 Combine apple, celery, onion and oil in 2-quart saucepan. Cook over medium heat for 4 to 8 minutes, or until apple is tender, stirring frequently. Remove from heat. Add bread crumbs, parsley and sage. Mix well.

3 Heat oven to 325°F. Untie pork roast. Separate the 2 pieces of loin. Spoon and pack apple mixture on top of 1 piece. Place remaining piece over stuffing. Tie at 1½-inch intervals to secure.

4 Place roast on rack in broiler pan. Roast for 1 hour 40 minutes to 1 hour 50 minutes, or until internal temperature registers 155°F and juices run clear, basting with glaze during last 15 minutes. Let stand, tented with foil, for 10 minutes. (Internal temperature will rise 5°F during standing.)

Nutrition Facts	Amount/serving	%DV*	Amount/serving	%DV*
Serving Size 1/12 roast (106g)	Total Fat 9g	14%	Total Carbohydrate 11g	4%
	Saturated Fat 3g	14%	Dietary Fiber <1g	3%
Servings per Recipe 12	Cholesterol 55mg	18%	Sugars 7g	
Calories 209	Sodium 91mg	4%	Protein 20g	
Calories from Fat 83	Vitamin A 2% • Vitamin C 6% • Calcium 4% • Iron 8%			

*Percent Daily Values (DV) are based on a 2000 calorie diet.

Menu Planning Guide

One serving of this recipe provides:

1 Meat, Poultry & Fish

Diet Exchanges:

½ starch • 2½ lean meat

Baked Corn Dogs

Serve with Dilled Barley Salad (p 96) and fresh fruit or applesauce

1 teaspoon yellow cornmeal

Dough:

1⅔ cups all-purpose flour

⅓ cup yellow cornmeal

3 tablespoons sugar

1 teaspoon baking powder

¼ teaspoon salt

⅔ cup warm water

1 tablespoon plus 1 teaspoon vegetable oil

10 flat wooden Popsicle sticks

1 pkg. (16 oz.) low-fat beef franks

2 tablespoons skim milk

10 servings

1 Heat oven to 350°F. Spray baking sheet with nonstick vegetable cooking spray. Sprinkle evenly with 1 teaspoon cornmeal. Set aside.

2 Combine flour, ⅓ cup cornmeal, the sugar, baking powder and salt in medium mixing bowl. Add water and oil. Stir until dough pulls away from side of bowl. Turn dough out onto lightly floured surface. Knead for 3 to 5 minutes, or until smooth and elastic. Cover dough with bowl. Let rest for 10 minutes.

3 Insert 1 wooden stick halfway into end of each frank. Set aside. Divide dough equally into 10 pieces. (Cover pieces with plastic wrap to prevent them from drying out.)

4 Roll 1 piece dough into 5 x 3-inch rectangle. Wrap rectangle around 1 frank, pressing edges tightly to seal. Place prepared corn dog seam-side-down on prepared baking sheet. Repeat with remaining dough and franks. (Cover prepared corn dogs with plastic wrap to prevent them from drying out.)

5 Brush tops and sides of corn dogs evenly with milk. Bake for 30 to 35 minutes, or until golden brown. (Corn dogs may split on one side.) Serve corn dogs with mustard, catsup and relish, if desired.

Nutrition Facts	Amount/serving	%DV*	Amount/serving	%DV*
Serving Size 1 corn dog (96g)	Total Fat 4g	6%	Total Carbohydrate 28g	9%
Servings per Recipe 10	Saturated Fat 1g	4%	Dietary Fiber 1g	4%
Calories 176	Cholesterol 20mg	7%	Sugars 6g	
Calories from Fat 32	Sodium 525mg	22%	Protein 9g	
	Vitamin A 0% • Vitamin C 6% • Calcium 6% • Iron 8%			
	*Percent Daily Values (DV) are based on a 2000 calorie diet.			

Menu Planning Guide

One serving of this recipe provides:

½ Meat, Poultry & Fish
1 Bread, Cereal, Rice & Pasta

Diet Exchanges:
1 lean meat • 1½ starch

Baked Pork Schnitzel

Serve with German Potato Salad (p 80)
and cabbage slaw or chunky applesauce

1-lb well-trimmed pork tenderloin, cut into
    1/2-inch slices
1/2 cup all-purpose flour
1/2 teaspoon pepper
1/4 teaspoon salt
1/2 cup frozen cholesterol-free egg product,
    defrosted; or 2 eggs, beaten
1 cup unseasoned dry bread crumbs
2 tablespoons snipped fresh parsley
1 lemon, thinly sliced

4 servings

1 Heat oven to 400°F. Spray baking sheet with nonstick vegetable cooking spray. Set aside. Pound tenderloin slices to 1/4 inch.

2 Combine flour, pepper and salt in shallow dish. Place egg product in second shallow dish. Place crumbs on sheet of wax paper. Dredge pork slices in flour mixture to coat. Dip slices in egg product, then dredge in crumbs to coat.

3 Arrange pork slices on prepared baking sheet. Lightly spray slices with nonstick vegetable cooking spray. Bake for 10 minutes.

4 Turn pork slices over. Spray with nonstick vegetable cooking spray. Bake for 10 to 12 minutes, or until slices are golden brown. Garnish pork schnitzel with parsley. Serve with lemon slices.

Nutrition Facts

Serving Size
  4 to 6 slices (174g)
Servings
  per Recipe 4
Calories 319
  Calories
  from Fat 51

Amount/serving	%DV*	Amount/serving	%DV*
Total Fat 6g	9%	Total Carbohydrate 32g	11%
Saturated Fat 2g	9%	Dietary Fiber 2g	8%
Cholesterol 73mg	24%	Sugars 2g	
Sodium 417mg	17%	Protein 33g	

Vitamin A 8% • Vitamin C 20% • Calcium 6% • Iron 20%
*Percent Daily Values (DV) are based on a 2000 calorie diet.

Menu Planning Guide
One serving of this recipe provides:
  1 Meat, Poultry & Fish
  2 Bread, Cereal, Rice & Pasta

Diet Exchanges:
3 lean meat • 2 starch

Chinese Five-Spice Ribs

Serve with steamed broccoli spears or steamed mixed vegetables

Sauce:

1½ cups apricot nectar
3 tablespoons cider vinegar
2 tablespoons packed brown sugar
2 tablespoons cornstarch
1 tablespoon tomato paste
1 teaspoon soy sauce
1 teaspoon grated fresh gingerroot
1 clove garlic, minced
½ teaspoon five-spice powder
⅛ teaspoon cayenne

1½ lbs. russet potatoes, cut into 1-inch chunks
2 lbs. well-trimmed bone-in pork loin back ribs, cut into 3-rib pieces

6 servings

Tip: If desired, reheat reserved sauce in 1-quart saucepan over low heat just until hot, stirring constantly.

1 Heat oven to 350°F. Spray rack in roasting pan with nonstick vegetable cooking spray. Set aside. In 2-quart saucepan, combine sauce ingredients. Cook over medium heat for 5 to 7 minutes, or until sauce is thickened and translucent, stirring constantly. Reserve ½ cup sauce. Set remaining sauce aside.

2 Cut two 20 x 12-inch pieces of foil. Place one piece on top of second. Place potatoes on foil. Pour ½ cup remaining sauce over potatoes, stirring gently to coat. Fold opposite sides of foil together in locked folds. Fold and crimp ends. Set aside.

3 Arrange ribs on prepared rack in roasting pan. Place pan on center rack in oven, and foil packet on lower rack. Bake for 45 minutes. Brush both sides of ribs with some of remaining sauce. Bake for additional 45 minutes, brushing ribs with remaining sauce every 15 minutes. Transfer ribs to serving platter. Cover to keep warm. Set aside.

4 Open potato packet and spread potatoes into single layer. Place under broiler with surface of potatoes 5 to 6 inches from heat. Broil for 4 to 6 minutes, or until potatoes are lightly browned. Serve ribs and potatoes with ½ cup reserved sauce.

Nutrition Facts	Amount/serving	%DV*	Amount/serving	%DV*
Serving Size ⅙ recipe (246g)	Total Fat 9g	14%	Total Carbohydrate 35g	12%
Servings per Recipe 6	Saturated Fat 4g	18%	Dietary Fiber 2g	7%
Calories 325	Cholesterol 57mg	19%	Sugars 15g	
Calories from Fat 83	Sodium 125mg	5%	Protein 25g	
	Vitamin A 20% • Vitamin C 20% • Calcium 4% • Iron 10%			
	*Percent Daily Values (DV) are based on a 2000 calorie diet.			

Menu Planning Guide

One serving of this recipe provides:
1 Meat, Poultry & Fish
1 Vegetable
½ Fruit

Diet Exchanges:

3 lean meat • 1½ starch • ½ fruit

Spinach Meatloaf with Fresh Tomato Sauce

Serve with Ricotta Polenta (p 106) or Garlic Mashed Potatoes (p 79)

Meatloaf:

1 cup boiling water

1/2 cup chopped sun-dried tomatoes (dry pack)

1 lb. lean ground beef, crumbled

1 pkg. (10 oz.) frozen chopped spinach, defrosted and well drained

1 medium onion, finely chopped (1 cup)

1/2 cup fresh bread crumbs

1/3 cup skim milk

1/4 cup frozen cholesterol-free egg product, defrosted; or 1 egg, beaten

2 tablespoons snipped fresh basil

1/2 teaspoon pepper

1/2 teaspoon salt (optional)

Sauce:

1 tablespoon olive oil

1 small onion, chopped (1/2 cup)

1 clove garlic, minced

5 Roma tomatoes, coarsely chopped (about 2 cups)

2 tablespoons tomato paste

1 tablespoon snipped fresh basil

1 teaspoon sugar

1/2 teaspoon pepper

6 servings

Tip: Since the spinach may make it difficult to slice the meatloaf smoothly, use a serrated knife, or finely chop the spinach before adding to meatloaf ingredients.

1 Heat oven to 350°F. In small mixing bowl, combine water and sun-dried tomatoes. Let stand for 15 minutes. Drain well.

2 Combine tomatoes and remaining meatloaf ingredients in large mixing bowl. Shape mixture to fit 8 1/2 x 4 1/2-inch loaf dish. Place in dish. Bake for 45 to 50 minutes, or until meatloaf pulls away from sides of dish and is firm. Let stand for 10 minutes before removing from dish and slicing.

3 Meanwhile, heat oil in 1-quart saucepan over medium heat. Add onion and garlic. Cook for 3 to 5 minutes, or until onion is tender, stirring frequently. Add tomatoes. Cook for 3 to 5 minutes, or until tomatoes release some liquid. Add remaining sauce ingredients. Reduce heat to low. Simmer sauce for 10 to 15 minutes, or until flavors are blended. Serve sauce over sliced meatloaf.

Nutrition Facts	Amount/serving	%DV*	Amount/serving	%DV*
Serving Size 1 slice with sauce (225g)	Total Fat 5g	8%	Total Carbohydrate 17g	6%
	Saturated Fat 1g	6%	Dietary Fiber 3g	12%
Servings per Recipe 6	Cholesterol 28mg	9%	Sugars 8g	
Calories 165 Calories from Fat 44	Sodium 328mg	14%	Protein 16g	
	Vitamin A 60% • Vitamin C 35% • Calcium 10% • Iron 20%			
	*Percent Daily Values (DV) are based on a 2000 calorie diet.			

Menu Planning Guide

One serving of this recipe provides:

1 Meat, Poultry & Fish
2 Vegetable

Diet Exchanges:

2 lean meat • 3 vegetable

Garlic-Herb Veal Roast

Serve with Carrots Gremolata (p 74)
and mashed potatoes or steamed new potatoes

1 *well-trimmed boneless veal roast (2 lbs.),*
   rolled and tied

1 *clove garlic, peeled and thinly slivered*

2 *tablespoons fresh lemon juice*

¼ *cup snipped fresh herbs (rosemary, parsley,*
   thyme, tarragon)*

1 *tablespoon Dijon mustard*

1 *teaspoon coarsely ground pepper*

¼ *cup water*

¼ *cup ready-to-serve chicken broth, dry white*
   wine or water

1 *tablespoon flour mixed with ¾ cup water*

8 servings

*Equal amounts of herbs are not necessary.
Blend them as desired.

1 Heat oven to 425°F. With sharp knife, make several small slits in top of roast. Place 1 garlic sliver in each slit. Sprinkle roast with juice. Set aside.

2 Combine herbs, mustard and pepper in small mixing bowl. Rub mixture over top and sides of roast. Place roast in shallow roasting pan. Pour water into pan around roast. Bake for 15 minutes. Reduce heat to 325°F. Insert meat thermometer into roast. Cover roast loosely with foil. Bake for additional 1½ to 2 hours (medium, 155°F), or until desired doneness. Transfer roast to serving platter. Cover to keep warm. Set aside.

3 Skim and discard fat from pan drippings. Stir in broth, scraping bottom of pan to loosen any browned bits. Place pan over medium heat. Whisk in flour mixture. Cook for 1 to 2 minutes, or until gravy is thickened, stirring constantly. Serve gravy with roast.

Corn Bread Stuffed Pork Tenderloin

Serve with Beans with Red Pepper Purée (p 73) and corn bread

Stuffing:

  1 teaspoon vegetable oil
 1/4 cup finely chopped onion
  2 tablespoons finely chopped celery
  1 clove garlic, minced
 1/2 cup day-old corn bread, crumbled
 1/4 cup frozen corn, defrosted and drained
 1/4 cup frozen cholesterol-free egg product,
      defrosted; or 1 egg, beaten
  1 tablespoon diced canned mild green chilies
 1/2 teaspoon dried oregano leaves
 1/4 teaspoon dried rubbed sage leaves
 1/4 teaspoon salt

  1 - lb. well-trimmed pork tenderloin, split in
      half lengthwise
  1 tablespoon mild red jalapeño pepper jelly
      melted with 1 teaspoon water

4 servings

1 Heat oven to 325°F. Spray rack in broiler pan with nonstick vegetable cooking spray. Set aside. In 7-inch nonstick skillet, heat oil over medium heat. Add onion and celery. Cook for 2½ to 3½ minutes, or until vegetables are tender, stirring frequently. Add garlic. Cook for 1 minute, stirring constantly. Remove from heat.

2 Combine vegetable mixture and remaining stuffing ingredients in medium mixing bowl. Spoon and pack stuffing on one half of tenderloin. Place remaining half of tenderloin over stuffing. Secure with evenly spaced pieces of string.

3 Place tenderloin on prepared rack. Bake for 1 hour to 1 hour 10 minutes, or until desired doneness, brushing with jelly mixture during last 15 minutes. Let stand, tented with foil, for 10 minutes.

Nutrition Facts	Amount/serving	%DV*	Amount/serving	%DV*
	Total Fat 7g	10%	Total Carbohydrate 14g	5%
Serving Size 1/4 tenderloin (159g)	Saturated Fat 2g	9%	Dietary Fiber 1g	4%
Servings per Recipe 4	Cholesterol 77mg	26%	Sugars 4g	
Calories 233	Sodium 318mg	13%	Protein 28g	
Calories from Fat 59	Vitamin A 6% • Vitamin C 4% • Calcium 6% • Iron 10%			

*Percent Daily Values (DV) are based on a 2000 calorie diet.

Menu Planning Guide

One serving of this recipe provides:

  1 Meat, Poultry & Fish
 1/2 Bread, Cereal, Rice & Pasta

Diet Exchanges:

3 lean meat • 1 starch

Chicken & Potato Casserole

Serve with Spicy Glazed Carrots (p 86)
or a crisp green salad and crusty French bread

1 lb. red or white potatoes, cut into ¼-inch
   slices (about 3 cups)

1 cup water

3 whole boneless chicken breasts (8 to 10 oz.
   each), skin removed, cut into 2 x ¼-inch
   strips

2 tablespoons margarine

3 tablespoons all-purpose flour

2 cups 1% low-fat milk

1 tablespoon snipped fresh parsley

1 teaspoon dried rubbed sage leaves

1 teaspoon dried thyme leaves

¾ teaspoon salt

¼ teaspoon white pepper

1 large red pepper, roasted*, peeled, seeded
   and cut into 1-inch chunks

1 tablespoon shredded fresh Parmesan cheese
   (optional)

6 servings

*To roast pepper, place it under broiler with sur-
face 1 to 2 inches from heat. Broil for 11 to 15
minutes, or until pepper blisters and blackens,
turning pepper frequently. Place pepper in
paper or plastic bag. Seal bag. Let stand for
10 minutes. Proceed as directed.

If desired, use drained, jarred roasted red peppers.

1 Spray 12 x 8-inch baking dish with non-stick vegetable cooking spray. Set aside. In 3-quart saucepan, combine potatoes and water. Cover. Cook over medium-high heat for 13 to 15 minutes, or just until potatoes are tender. Drain. Set aside.

2 Cook chicken over medium heat in 10-inch nonstick skillet for 6 to 8 minutes, or until meat is no longer pink, stirring frequently. Drain. Set aside.

3 Heat oven to 350°F. Melt margarine in 1-quart saucepan over medium heat. Stir in flour. Cook for 2 minutes, stirring constantly. Gradually blend in milk. Stir in parsley, sage, thyme, salt and white pepper. Cook for 5 to 10 minutes, or until sauce thickens and bubbles, stirring constantly. Remove from heat. Set aside.

4 Layer half of potatoes, half of chicken and half of pepper chunks in prepared dish. Repeat layers. Pour sauce evenly over top. Sprinkle evenly with Parmesan cheese. Bake for 20 to 25 minutes, or until casserole is hot and edges are bubbly.

Nutrition Facts	Amount/serving	%DV*	Amount/serving	%DV*
Serving Size 1 cup (278g)	Total Fat 8g	12%	Total Carbohydrate 25g	8%
Servings per Recipe 6	Saturated Fat 2g	11%	Dietary Fiber 2g	8%
Calories 295	Cholesterol 75mg	25%	Sugars 6g	
Calories from Fat 70	Sodium 417mg	17%	Protein 31g	

Vitamin A 35% • Vitamin C 90% • Calcium 15% • Iron 10%

*Percent Daily Values (DV) are based on a 2000 calorie diet.

Menu Planning Guide

One serving of this recipe provides:

½ Milk, Yogurt & Cheese
1 Meat, Poultry & Fish
1 Vegetable

Diet Exchanges:

3 lean meat • ½ skim milk • 1 starch

Chicken Pot Pie

Serve with cooked rhubarb sauce or fresh fruit

½ cup warm water (105° to 115°F)

1 pkg. (¼ oz.) active dry yeast

½ teaspoon sugar

2½ cups plus 3 tablespoons all-purpose flour, divided

1 teaspoon grated lemon peel (optional)

½ teaspoon salt

⅓ cup frozen cholesterol-free egg product, defrosted; or 2 eggs, beaten

¼ cup plus 2 tablespoons nonfat plain yogurt cheese*

3 cups shredded cooked chicken breast

2 cups frozen mixed vegetables, defrosted and drained

2 tablespoons margarine or butter

1 teaspoon dried basil leaves

¾ teaspoon seasoned salt

½ teaspoon freshly ground pepper

2 cups skim milk

6 servings

*Make yogurt cheese by spooning gelatin-free yogurt into paper-towel-lined strainer. Place over bowl and let drain overnight in refrigerator.

1 Combine water, yeast and sugar in small bowl. Let stand for 5 minutes. In large mixing bowl, combine 2 cups flour, the peel and salt. Make a well in center and add yeast mixture, egg product and yogurt cheese. Stir until well blended. Stir in ½ cup flour with wooden spoon until completely incorporated. Shape dough into ball (dough will be sticky; add flour as necessary). Place ball into lightly floured large mixing bowl. Cover with cloth. Let rise in warm place for 45 minutes to 1 hour, or until double in size.

2 Spray 10-inch deep-dish pie plate with nonstick vegetable cooking spray. Divide dough in half. Cover half of dough with plastic wrap. Set aside. Press remaining dough into bottom and up sides of prepared plate, pinching to secure dough to top edge of plate. Spoon chicken into crust. Spread vegetables evenly over chicken. Set aside.

3 Heat oven to 350°F. In 1-quart saucepan, melt margarine over medium heat. Stir in remaining 3 tablespoons flour, the basil, seasoned salt and pepper. Cook for 2 minutes, stirring frequently. Gradually blend in milk. Cook for 12 to 14 minutes, or until sauce thickens and bubbles, stirring frequently. Pour sauce over chicken and vegetables.

4 Press remaining dough into 10-inch circle on floured wax paper. Place circle over filling. Remove and discard wax paper. Pinch edges to seal. With sharp knife, cut vents in top crust. Bake for 45 to 55 minutes, or until crust is golden brown.

Nutrition Facts	Amount/serving	%DV*	Amount/serving	%DV*
Serving Size 1 slice (316g)	Total Fat 7g	10%	Total Carbohydrate 56g	19%
Servings per Recipe 6	Saturated Fat 2g	8%	Dietary Fiber 5g	22%
Calories 424	Cholesterol 56mg	19%	Sugars 8g	
Calories from Fat 61	Sodium 535mg	22%	Protein 33g	
	Vitamin A 60% • Vitamin C 4% • Calcium 15% • Iron 25%			
	*Percent Daily Values (DV) are based on a 2000 calorie diet.			

Menu Planning Guide

One serving of this recipe provides:

½ Milk, Yogurt & Cheese
1 Meat, Poultry & Fish
1 Vegetable
3 Bread, Cereal, Rice & Pasta

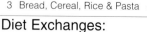

Diet Exchanges:

2½ lean meat • ½ skim milk • 3 starch • ½ vegetable

Lime & Cumin Cornish Game Hens

Serve with Carrots Gremolata (p 74) and steamed new potatoes

¼ cup dark corn syrup

½ to 1 teaspoon grated lime peel

2 tablespoons lime juice

1 teaspoon ground cumin, divided

4 Cornish game hens (24 oz. each)

½ teaspoon dried oregano leaves

¼ teaspoon salt

⅛ teaspoon pepper

8 servings

1 Combine syrup, peel, juice and ½ teaspoon cumin in small bowl. Set aside.

2 Secure hens' legs together with string. Place hens in large plastic food-storage bag. Pour syrup mixture over hens. Secure bag and place in dish. Refrigerate at least 2 hours, turning bag over once.

3 Heat oven to 350°F. Remove hens from marinade and arrange breast-side-up on rack in shallow roasting pan. Discard marinade. In small bowl, combine remaining ½ teaspoon cumin and remaining ingredients. Rub hens with mixture.

4 Bake for 45 minutes to 1 hour, or until internal temperature in thickest portions of thighs registers 175°F. Cut hens in half lengthwise before serving. Before eating, remove and discard skin.

Nutrition Facts	Amount/serving	%DV*	Amount/serving	%DV*
Serving Size ½ hen (117g) Servings per Recipe 8 Calories 195 Calories from Fat 69	Total Fat 8g	12%	Total Carbohydrate <1g	0%
	Saturated Fat 2g	11%	Dietary Fiber <1g	0%
	Cholesterol 87mg	29%	Sugars <1g	
	Sodium 154mg	6%	Protein 29g	
	Vitamin A 2% • Vitamin C 0% • Calcium 2% • Iron 8%			
	*Percent Daily Values (DV) are based on a 2000 calorie diet.			

Menu Planning Guide

One serving of this recipe provides:
1½ Meat, Poultry & Fish

Diet Exchanges:
4 lean meat

Oven "Fried" Chicken

Serve with corn on the cob and Dilled Barley Salad (p 92)
or Hominy Sausage Succotash (p 101)

½ cup plain nonfat or low-fat yogurt

Seasoning:

¼ cup all-purpose flour

¼ cup yellow cornmeal

2 teaspoons sugar

1 teaspoon dried oregano leaves

1 teaspoon dried basil leaves

½ teaspoon salt

½ teaspoon paprika

½ teaspoon dry mustard

½ teaspoon imitation butter-flavored sprinkles

¼ teaspoon garlic powder

¼ teaspoon onion powder

¼ teaspoon pepper

⅛ teaspoon cayenne

3 - lb. whole broiler-fryer chicken, cut into
8 pieces, skin removed

4 servings

1 Heat oven to 375°F. Spray baking sheet with nonstick vegetable cooking spray. Set aside. Place yogurt in shallow dish. Whisk until smooth. In second shallow dish, combine seasoning ingredients. Dredge chicken first in yogurt to lightly coat, then in seasoning to coat.

2 Place chicken on prepared baking sheet. Spray chicken with nonstick vegetable cooking spray. Bake for 40 to 45 minutes, or until chicken is golden brown, meat near bone is no longer pink and juices run clear.

Nutrition Facts	Amount/serving	%DV*	Amount/serving	%DV*
Serving Size 2 pieces (174g)	Total Fat 10g	15%	Total Carbohydrate 18g	6%
Servings per Recipe 4	Saturated Fat 3g	13%	Dietary Fiber 1g	5%
Calories 324	Cholesterol 110mg	37%	Sugars 5g	
Calories from Fat 86	Sodium 399mg	17%	Protein 39g	

Vitamin A 8% • Vitamin C 2% • Calcium 10% • Iron 15%
*Percent Daily Values (DV) are based on a 2000 calorie diet.

Menu Planning Guide

One serving of this recipe provides:
1½ Meat, Poultry & Fish
1 Bread, Cereal, Rice & Pasta

Diet Exchanges:

4½ lean meat • 1 starch

Roast Turkey Breast with Sweet & Sour Gravy

Serve with Ratatouille with Potatoes (p 83) or Garlic Mashed Potatoes (p 79) and Creamy Baby Lima Beans (p 77)

1 can (20 oz.) pineapple rings in juice,
    drained (reserve ¾ cup juice)

Baste:

1 cup ready-to-serve chicken broth

⅓ cup packed brown sugar

¼ cup additional pineapple juice

2 tablespoons cider vinegar

¾ teaspoon dry mustard

⅛ teaspoon ground cloves

1 bone-in whole turkey breast (5 lbs.), skin on

½ teaspoon vegetable oil

⅛ teaspoon pepper

1 cup water

1 tablespoon plus 1½ teaspoons cornstarch

10 servings

1 Heat oven to 450°F. Spray rack in roasting pan with nonstick vegetable cooking spray. Set aside. Set pineapple rings aside. In 2-cup measure, combine reserved juice and baste ingredients. Reserve ¾ cup baste. Set remaining baste aside.

2 Place turkey breast-side-up on prepared rack. Brush turkey evenly with oil. Sprinkle evenly with pepper. Pour water in bottom of roasting pan. Place pan in oven. Immediately reduce oven temperature to 325°F. Bake for 2 to 2½ hours, or until internal temperature in thickest part of breast registers 185°F, brushing turkey with ¾ cup reserved baste every 30 minutes and arranging pineapple rings around turkey during last 45 minutes.

3 Meanwhile, combine remaining baste and cornstarch in 1-quart saucepan. Cook over medium-low heat for 4 to 8 minutes, or until gravy is thickened and translucent, stirring constantly. Serve gravy with turkey. Garnish with pineapple rings. Before eating, remove and discard skin.

Nutrition Facts	Amount/serving	%DV*	Amount/serving	%DV*
Serving Size ¹⁄₁₀ recipe (208g)	Total Fat 4g	7%	Total Carbohydrate 18g	6%
Servings per Recipe 10	Saturated Fat 1g	6%	Dietary Fiber 0g	0%
Calories 257	Cholesterol 93mg	31%	Sugars 17g	
Calories from Fat 40	Sodium 162mg	7%	Protein 35g	
	Vitamin A 0% • Vitamin C 10% • Calcium 4% • Iron 8%			
	*Percent Daily Values (DV) are based on a 2000 calorie diet.			

Menu Planning Guide

One serving of this recipe provides:
1½ Meat, Poultry & Fish
½ Fruit

Diet Exchanges:
4 lean meat • ½ starch • ½ fruit

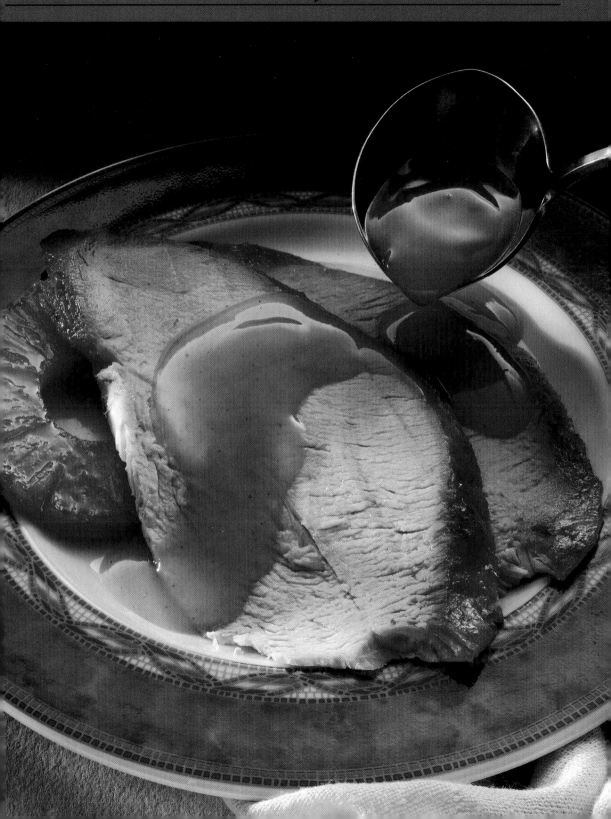

Roasted Mediterranean Chicken

Serve with Ratatouille with Potatoes (p 83)
or Mushroom & Lemon Penne (p 102) and steamed baby carrots

Marinade:

1 cup fresh orange juice

¾ cup finely chopped onion

1 tablespoon ground cumin

2 teaspoons dried oregano leaves

1½ teaspoons ground coriander

½ teaspoon ground cardamom

½ teaspoon ground allspice

2½ to 3-lb. whole broiler-fryer chicken, skin on

½ orange, cut into 3 wedges

½ small onion, cut into 3 wedges

1 sprig fresh oregano leaves

4 servings

1 Combine marinade ingredients in 2-cup measure. Reserve ⅓ cup marinade. Place remaining marinade in large plastic food-storage bag. Add chicken. Secure bag. Turn to coat. Chill at least 4 hours or overnight, turning bag occasionally.

2 Heat oven to 350°F. Spray rack in roasting pan with nonstick vegetable cooking spray. Set aside. Drain and discard marinade from chicken. Stuff cavity with orange and onion wedges. Secure legs with string. Place chicken breast-side-up in prepared pan. Tuck wing tips behind back.

3 Bake for 1½ to 2 hours, or until internal temperature in thickest portions of both thighs registers 185°F, basting chicken with reserved marinade during last 15 minutes of baking. Before serving, remove and discard skin and stuffing.

Nutrition Facts	Amount/serving	%DV*	Amount/serving	%DV*
Serving Size ¼ chicken (132g)	Total Fat 8g	12%	Total Carbohydrate 4g	1%
Servings per Recipe 4	Saturated Fat 2g	11%	Dietary Fiber 0g	0%
Calories 207	Cholesterol 89mg	30%	Sugars 3g	
Calories from Fat 69	Sodium 88mg	4%	Protein 29g	

Vitamin A 2% • Vitamin C 20% • Calcium 4% • Iron 10%

*Percent Daily Values (DV) are based on a 2000 calorie diet.

Menu Planning Guide

One serving of this recipe provides:

1 Meat, Poultry & Fish

Diet Exchanges:

3½ lean meat

Fruit-stuffed Turkey Tenderloins

Serve with Sautéed Peppers in Tarragon Vinaigrette (p 84) and a whole wheat roll

Stuffing:

- 1 can (8 oz.) crushed pineapple in juice, drained
- 1/2 cup chopped red cooking apple
- 1/3 cup cooked long-grain white rice
- 1/4 cup canned mandarin orange segments in light syrup, drained
- 2 tablespoons raisins
- 1 tablespoon snipped fresh chives
- 2 teaspoons soy sauce
- 1/2 teaspoon ground coriander

- 2 turkey tenderloins (8 oz. each)
- 1/4 teaspoon pepper
- 2 tablespoons orange marmalade
- 1/2 teaspoon toasted sesame seed

4 servings

1 Heat oven to 350°F. In small mixing bowl, combine stuffing ingredients. Set aside. Slit each tenderloin lengthwise to within 1/2 inch of edge to form pocket. Rub inside of pockets evenly with pepper. Fill pockets evenly with stuffing.

2 Arrange tenderloins in 8-inch square baking dish. Brush tops of tenderloins evenly with marmalade. Sprinkle tenderloins evenly with sesame seed. Cover dish with foil. Bake for 35 to 40 minutes, or until meat is no longer pink and juices run clear. Cut tenderloins in half crosswise before serving.

Nutrition Facts	Amount/serving	%DV*	Amount/serving	%DV*
Serving Size 1/2 tenderloin (199g)	Total Fat 2g	2%	Total Carbohydrate 25g	8%
Servings per Recipe 4	Saturated Fat <1g	2%	Dietary Fiber 2g	6%
Calories 220	Cholesterol 72mg	24%	Sugars 18g	
Calories from Fat 14	Sodium 227mg	9%	Protein 27g	

Vitamin A 4% • Vitamin C 25% • Calcium 4% • Iron 10%

*Percent Daily Values (DV) are based on a 2000 calorie diet.

Menu Planning Guide

One serving of this recipe provides:

1 Meat, Poultry & Fish
1 Fruit

Diet Exchanges:

3 lean meat • 1/2 starch • 1 fruit

Baked Red Snapper

Serve with Cajun Dirty Rice (p 95) and a mixed green salad

1-lb. red snapper fillet, cut into serving-size
  pieces, 3/4 inch thick

1/2 cup chopped shallots

1 clove garlic, minced

1 teaspoon olive oil

1/4 cup fresh lemon juice

1/4 cup snipped fresh parsley

1/2 teaspoon paprika

1/2 teaspoon ground cumin

1/8 teaspoon freshly ground pepper

8 tomato slices

4 servings

1 Heat oven to 350°F. Spray 8-inch square baking dish with nonstick vegetable cooking spray. Arrange snapper skin-side-down in dish. Set aside.

2 Combine shallots, garlic and oil in 10-inch nonstick skillet. Cook over medium heat for 3 to 4 minutes, or until shallots are tender-crisp, stirring frequently. Remove from heat. Stir in juice, parsley, paprika, cumin and pepper.

3 Pour shallot mixture over snapper. Arrange tomato slices evenly over snapper. Cover dish with foil. Bake for 20 to 25 minutes, or until fish is firm and opaque and just begins to flake. Serve on spinach-lined serving plates.

Nutrition Facts	Amount/serving	%DV*	Amount/serving	%DV*
	Total Fat 3g	4%	Total Carbohydrate 7g	2%
Serving Size 1 piece (152g)	Saturated Fat 1g	3%	Dietary Fiber 1g	4%
Servings per Recipe 4	Cholesterol 42mg	14%	Sugars 3g	
Calories 151	Sodium 58mg	2%	Protein 24g	
Calories from Fat 26	Vitamin A 70% • Vitamin C 35% • Calcium 6% • Iron 6%			
	*Percent Daily Values (DV) are based on a 2000 calorie diet.			

Menu Planning Guide
One serving of this recipe provides:

1 Meat, Poultry & Fish
1 Vegetable

Diet Exchanges:
3 lean meat • 1 vegetable

Crabmeat Quiche with Orzo Crust

Serve with Creamy Baby Lima Beans (p 77)
or steamed mixed vegetables

Crust:

1 *cup uncooked orzo pasta (rosamarina)*

2 *egg whites, slightly beaten*

1 *teaspoon dried dill weed*

1/2 *teaspoon dry mustard*

2 *cups frozen broccoli, cauliflower and carrots*

1/4 *cup finely chopped shallots*

1/4 *cup water*

1 *cup frozen cholesterol-free egg product, defrosted, or 4 eggs*

1 *can (6 oz.) crabmeat, rinsed and drained*

1/3 *cup shredded reduced-fat Swiss cheese*

1/4 *cup skim milk*

1/2 *teaspoon salt*

1/4 *teaspoon cayenne*

6 servings

1 Heat oven to 350°F. Spray 9-inch deep-dish pie plate with nonstick vegetable cooking spray. Set aside. Prepare orzo as directed on package. Rinse and drain. In medium mixing bowl, combine orzo and remaining crust ingredients. Using back of spoon, press crust against bottom and sides of prepared plate. Bake for 20 to 22 minutes, or until crust is set and begins to brown. Set aside.

2 Combine vegetables, shallots and water in 2-quart saucepan. Cover. Cook over medium heat for 4 to 7 minutes, or until vegetables are hot and shallots are tender-crisp, stirring occasionally. Drain.

3 Stir in remaining ingredients. Mix well. Pour into prepared crust. Bake for 35 to 38 minutes, or until knife inserted in center comes out clean. Let stand for 10 minutes before slicing into wedges.

Nutrition Facts	Amount/serving	%DV*	Amount/serving	%DV*
	Total Fat 1g	2%	Total Carbohydrate 12g	4%
Serving Size 1 wedge (157g)	Saturated Fat <1g	2%	Dietary Fiber 2g	8%
Servings per Recipe 6	Cholesterol 25mg	8%	Sugars 3g	
Calories 118	Sodium 378mg	16%	Protein 14g	
Calories from Fat 13	Vitamin A 100% • Vitamin C 25% • Calcium 15% • Iron 8%			
	*Percent Daily Values (DV) are based on a 2000 calorie diet.			

Menu Planning Guide

One serving of this recipe provides:

1/2 Meat, Poultry & Fish
1/2 Vegetable
1/2 Bread, Cereal, Rice & Pasta

Diet Exchanges:

1 1/2 lean meat • 1/2 starch • 1/2 vegetable

Fillet of Sole Almondine

Serve with Creamy Baby Lima Beans (p 77) and Vegetable Couscous (p 108)

4 *thin red onion slices*
6 *thin lemon slices*
¼ *cup sliced green onions*
2 *tablespoons sliced almonds*
2 *fillets sole or other lean, white fish*
    (4 oz. each), ½ inch thick

⅛ *teaspoon salt*
⅛ *teaspoon white or lemon pepper*
    Paprika

2 servings

1 Heat oven to 350°F. Spray 12 x 8-inch baking dish with nonstick vegetable cooking spray. Arrange 2 slices each of red onion and lemon in dish. Sprinkle with half of green onions and 1 tablespoon almonds.

2 Arrange fillets in single layer over onions, lemon and almonds. Sprinkle lightly with salt, pepper and paprika. Top with remaining red onion, lemon, green onions and almonds. Cover dish with foil. Bake for 25 to 28 minutes, or until fish is firm and opaque and just begins to flake.

Nutrition Facts	Amount/serving	%DV*	Amount/serving	%DV*
Serving Size 1 fillet (160g)	Total Fat 6g	9%	Total Carbohydrate 7g	2%
Servings per Recipe 2	Saturated Fat <1g	4%	Dietary Fiber 2g	8%
Calories 175	Cholesterol 60mg	20%	Sugars 4g	
Calories from Fat 53	Sodium 230mg	10%	Protein 24g	

Vitamin A 2% • Vitamin C 30% • Calcium 6% • Iron 6%
*Percent Daily Values (DV) are based on a 2000 calorie diet.

Menu Planning Guide
One serving of this recipe provides:
1 Meat, Poultry & Fish
½ Vegetable

Diet Exchanges:
3 lean meat • ½ vegetable

Japanese Marinated Salmon Fillet

Serve with Gingered Japanese Noodles (p 99)
or hot cooked brown rice and steamed snow pea pods

1 - *lb. salmon fillet (³⁄₄ inch thick), cut into*
    4 serving-size pieces

Marinade:

2 *tablespoons reduced-sodium soy sauce*

1 *tablespoon lemon juice*

1 *tablespoon packed brown sugar*

1 *clove garlic, minced*

½ *cup thinly sliced leek*

1 *medium carrot, cut into 2 x ¹⁄₈-inch*
    strips (½ cup)

2 *cups hot cooked brown rice*

4 servings

1 Arrange salmon skin-side-up in 8-inch square baking dish. Set aside. In 1-cup measure, combine marinade ingredients. Stir until sugar is dissolved. Pour marinade over salmon, turning salmon over once to coat. Cover dish with plastic wrap. Chill 1 hour.

2 Remove and discard plastic wrap. Heat oven to 375°F. Arrange leek and carrot evenly on salmon. Cover dish with foil. Bake for 15 to 20 minutes, or until fish is firm and opaque and just begins to flake. Serve with rice.

Nutrition Facts	Amount/serving	%DV*	Amount/serving	%DV*
Serving Size 1 fillet with rice (231g)	Total Fat 8g	12%	Total Carbohydrate 29g	10%
Servings per Recipe 4	Saturated Fat 2g	8%	Dietary Fiber 3g	12%
Calories 296	Cholesterol 65mg	22%	Sugars 4g	
Calories from Fat 73	Sodium 370mg	15%	Protein 26g	

Vitamin A 80% • Vitamin C 4% • Calcium 4% • Iron 10%
*Percent Daily Values (DV) are based on a 2000 calorie diet.

Menu Planning Guide
One serving of this recipe provides:
  1 Meat, Poultry & Fish
  ½ Vegetable
  1 Bread, Cereal, Rice & Pasta

Diet Exchanges:
3 lean meat • 1½ starch • ½ vegetable

Mock Fried Fish

Serve with Cajun Dirty Rice (p 95) and steamed green beans

1 egg white
1 tablespoon water
¼ cup all-purpose flour
¼ cup yellow cornmeal
1 teaspoon dried oregano leaves
½ teaspoon dried basil leaves
½ teaspoon paprika
½ teaspoon ground coriander
¼ teaspoon salt
⅛ teaspoon cayenne (optional)
1½ lbs. fresh cod or other firm white fish,
    cut into 6 serving-size pieces (¾ to
    1 inch thick)
1 lemon, cut into 6 wedges

6 servings

1 Heat oven to 350°F. Spray baking sheet with nonstick vegetable cooking spray. Set aside. In shallow dish, lightly beat egg white with water. In second shallow dish, combine flour, cornmeal, oregano, basil, paprika, coriander, salt and cayenne.

2 Dip fish first in egg white mixture, then dredge in flour mixture to coat. Place fish on prepared baking sheet. Spray fish with nonstick vegetable cooking spray.

3 Bake for 20 to 25 minutes, or until fish is firm and opaque and just begins to flake, turning fish over after half the time and spraying again with nonstick vegetable cooking spray. Serve fish with lemon wedges.

Nutrition Facts	Amount/serving	%DV*	Amount/serving	%DV*
Serving Size 1 piece fish (108g)	Total Fat 1g	1%	Total Carbohydrate 10g	3%
	Saturated Fat 0g	0%	Dietary Fiber <1g	4%
Servings per Recipe 6	Cholesterol 43mg	14%	Sugars 1g	
Calories 130	Sodium 169mg	7%	Protein 20g	
Calories from Fat 9	Vitamin A 4% • Vitamin C 10% • Calcium 2% • Iron 6%			
	*Percent Daily Values (DV) are based on a 2000 calorie diet.			

Menu Planning Guide
One serving of this recipe provides:
1 Meat, Poultry & Fish
½ Bread, Cereal, Rice & Pasta

Diet Exchanges:
2½ lean meat • ½ starch

Rosemary Rainbow Trout

Serve with Mushroom & Lemon Penne (p 102)
or Garlic Mashed Potatoes (p 79)

6 *whole drawn stream trout (8 oz. each)*

½ *teaspoon salt*

½ *teaspoon pepper*

6 *sprigs fresh rosemary (2 inches long)*

2 *teaspoons olive oil*

Lemon wedges (optional)

6 servings

1 Place oven rack in center of oven. Heat oven to 400°F. Cut six 15 x 10-inch sheets of kitchen parchment. Set aside.

2 Sprinkle cavities of trout evenly with salt and pepper. Place 1 sprig rosemary in each cavity. Brush outsides of trout evenly with oil. Spray one side of each parchment paper sheet with nonstick vegetable cooking spray.

3 Place 1 trout in center of each sheet. Roll up each trout in paper, twisting ends to seal. Place packets directly on center oven rack, spacing at least 1 inch apart. Bake for 15 to 20 minutes, or until fish begins to flake when fork is inserted at backbone in thickest part of fish. Using scissors, cut packets down center to open. Remove and discard skin before eating. Serve with lemon wedges.

Nutrition Facts	Amount/serving	%DV*	Amount/serving	%DV*	Menu Planning Guide
Serving Size 1 trout (109g)	Total Fat 7g	10%	Total Carbohydrate 0g	0%	One serving of this recipe provides:
Servings per Recipe 6	Saturated Fat 2g	9%	Dietary Fiber 0g	0%	1 Meat, Poultry & Fish
Calories 170	Cholesterol 74mg	25%	Sugars 0g		
Calories from Fat 59	Sodium 238mg	10%	Protein 25g		
	Vitamin A 2% • Vitamin C 4% • Calcium 10% • Iron 4%				
	*Percent Daily Values (DV) are based on a 2000 calorie diet.				

Diet Exchanges:
3 lean meat

Stuffed Rainbow Trout

Serve with hot cooked wild rice and steamed broccoli spears

Stuffing:

¼ cup finely chopped onion

¼ cup finely chopped red pepper

¼ cup finely chopped green pepper

1½ cups day-old French bread cubes
    (¼-inch cubes)

1 can (4½ oz.) small deveined shrimp,
    rinsed and drained

½ cup frozen cholesterol-free egg product,
    defrosted; or 2 eggs, slightly beaten

1 tablespoon snipped fresh cilantro leaves

¼ teaspoon salt (optional)

⅛ teaspoon cayenne

4 whole drawn stream trout (8 oz. each),
    heads removed

2 teaspoons olive oil

⅛ teaspoon pepper

4 servings

1 Heat oven to 375°F. Spray 10-inch non-stick skillet with nonstick vegetable cooking spray. Add onion and chopped peppers. Cook for 2 to 3 minutes, or until tender-crisp, stirring frequently. In medium mixing bowl, combine onion mixture and remaining stuffing ingredients. Set aside.

2 Brush exteriors and cavities of fish evenly with oil. Sprinkle cavities evenly with pepper. Spray 8-inch square baking dish with nonstick vegetable cooking spray.

3 Arrange trout cavity-sides-up in prepared dish (use crushed pieces of foil between fish as necessary to keep fish propped upright). Stuff each fish evenly with stuffing mixture. Bake for 20 to 23 minutes, or until fish is firm and opaque and just begins to flake.

Nutrition Facts	Amount/serving	%DV*	Amount/serving	%DV*	Menu Planning Guide
Serving Size 1 trout (158g)	Total Fat 9g	13%	Total Carbohydrate 9g	3%	One serving of this recipe provides:
	Saturated Fat 1g	7%	Dietary Fiber 1g	4%	1 Meat, Poultry & Fish
Servings per Recipe 4	Cholesterol 94mg	31%	Sugars 2g		½ Bread, Cereal, Rice & Pasta
Calories 224	Sodium 191mg	8%	Protein 27g		
Calories from Fat 78	Vitamin A 15% • Vitamin C 35% • Calcium 8% • Iron 15%				
	*Percent Daily Values (DV) are based on a 2000 calorie diet.				

Diet Exchanges:
3 lean meat • ½ starch

Baked Spinach Fettucini

Serve with Spicy Glazed Carrots (p 86) or a tossed green salad

1 pkg. (9 oz.) fresh spinach fettucini,
    cut into quarters; or 8 oz. dry spinach
    fettucini, broken in half
¼ cup unseasoned dry bread crumbs, divided
1 cup frozen cholesterol-free egg product,
    defrosted; or 4 eggs, beaten
1 cup chopped red pepper
1 small onion, finely chopped (½ cup)

½ cup low-fat or nonfat ricotta cheese
¼ cup shredded fresh Parmesan cheese
1 tablespoon olive oil
2 teaspoons Italian seasoning
2 cloves garlic, minced
¾ teaspoon salt
¼ teaspoon white pepper

6 servings

1 Heat oven to 375°F. Prepare pasta as directed on package. Drain. Set aside. Spray 9-inch round baking dish with non-stick vegetable cooking spray. Sprinkle inside of dish with 2 tablespoons bread crumbs, tilting dish to coat sides. Repeat with nonstick vegetable cooking spray and remaining 2 tablespoons bread crumbs. Set crust aside. Combine remaining ingredients, except pasta, in large mixing bowl. Add pasta to pepper mixture. Stir to combine.

2 Slide pasta mixture evenly into prepared dish. Spray piece of foil with nonstick vegetable cooking spray. Cover dish with foil. Bake for 45 to 50 minutes, or until crust is deep golden brown. Remove foil. Bake for additional 10 to 15 minutes, or until knife inserted in center comes out clean. (Surface may appear slightly moist.) Loosen sides of fettucini with spatula or knife. Invert dish onto serving plate. (Do not remove dish.) Let stand for 10 minutes. Gently remove dish. Serve fettucini in wedges. Serve with hot, low-fat pasta sauce, if desired.

Nutrition Facts	Amount/serving	%DV*	Amount/serving	%DV*
Serving Size 1 wedge (206g)	Total Fat 6g	9%	Total Carbohydrate 35g	12%
Servings per Recipe 6	Saturated Fat 2g	10%	Dietary Fiber 3g	10%
Calories 250	Cholesterol 11mg	4%	Sugars 3g	
Calories from Fat 55	Sodium 427mg	18%	Protein 13g	

Vitamin A 30% • Vitamin C 60% • Calcium 15% • Iron 10%
*Percent Daily Values (DV) are based on a 2000 calorie diet.

Menu Planning Guide
One serving of this recipe provides:
½ Milk, Yogurt & Cheese
½ Vegetable
2 Bread, Cereal, Rice & Pasta

Diet Exchanges:
1 lean meat • 2 starch • ½ vegetable

Bean Cassoulet

*Serve with crusty French bread and a mixed greens salad
or Sautéed Peppers in Tarragon Vinaigrette (p 84)*

2 teaspoons olive oil

1 medium yellow squash, sliced (1 cup)

1 small leek, chopped (1 cup)

1/2 cup chopped fresh mushrooms

1/2 cup thinly sliced fennel bulb ✓

1 medium carrot, chopped (1/2 cup)

1 clove garlic, minced

1 can (15 1/2 oz.) Great Northern beans,
    rinsed and drained

1 can (15 1/2 oz.) pinto beans, rinsed and drained

1 can (14 1/2 oz.) no-salt-added whole tomatoes,
    undrained, cut up

1/2 to 1 teaspoon dried thyme leaves

1 teaspoon dried basil leaves

1 teaspoon pepper

1/2 teaspoon salt

1/4 cup unseasoned dry bread crumbs

1 tablespoon margarine or butter, melted

6 servings

*Note: A cassoulet is a classic French specialty
made with white beans and, usually, a variety of
meats. It is cooked slowly to blend the flavors.*

1 Heat oven to 350°F. In 4-quart saucepan,
heat oil over medium-high heat. Add
squash, leek, mushrooms, fennel, carrot and
garlic. Cook for 5 to 7 minutes, or until fennel is tender-crisp, stirring frequently.

2 Stir in beans, tomatoes, thyme, basil,
pepper and salt. Spoon mixture into
2-quart casserole.

3 Bake for 40 to 45 minutes, or until cassoulet is bubbly around edges. Remove
from oven. In small mixing bowl, combine
bread crumbs and margarine. Sprinkle mixture evenly over cassoulet. Place under
broiler with surface of cassoulet 4 to 5 inches from heat. Broil for 2 to 3 minutes, or
until top is golden brown.

Nutrition Facts	Amount/serving	%DV*	Amount/serving	%DV*
Serving Size approximately 1 cup (282g)	Total Fat 5g	7%	Total Carbohydrate 43g	14%
Servings per Recipe 6	Saturated Fat 1g	4%	Dietary Fiber 14g	55%
Calories 253	Cholesterol 0mg	0%	Sugars 6g	
Calories from Fat 41	Sodium 254mg	11%	Protein 13g	

Vitamin A 120% • Vitamin C 35% • Calcium 15% • Iron 25%

*Percent Daily Values (DV) are based on a 2000 calorie diet.

Menu Planning Guide
One serving of this recipe provides:
1/2 Meat, Poultry & Fish
1 Vegetable

Diet Exchanges:
2 1/2 starch • 1 vegetable • 1/2 fat

Cheesy Vegetable & Egg Casserole

Serve with English muffins with jam and a grapefruit half

1½ cups water

½ cup uncooked converted white rice

2 teaspoons low-sodium chicken bouillon granules

¾ cup frozen cholesterol-free egg product, defrosted; or 3 eggs, lightly beaten

½ cup finely chopped red pepper

1 small onion, chopped (½ cup)

½ teaspoon dried basil leaves

½ teaspoon dried oregano leaves

⅛ to ¼ teaspoon cayenne

⅛ teaspoon freshly ground pepper

1 pkg. (10 oz.) frozen artichoke hearts or broccoli, defrosted, drained and coarsely chopped

¾ cup shredded reduced-fat Cheddar cheese

4 servings

1 Heat oven to 350°F. Spray 8-inch square baking dish with nonstick vegetable cooking spray. Set aside. In 1-quart saucepan, bring water to boil over high heat. Remove from heat. Add rice and bouillon, stirring to dissolve granules. Set aside.

2 Whisk egg product lightly in large mixing bowl. Stir in red pepper, onion, basil, oregano, cayenne and ground pepper. Add rice mixture, artichoke hearts and cheese. Stir to combine.

3 Spread mixture evenly in prepared dish. Cover dish tightly with foil. Bake for 45 minutes. Uncover. Bake for additional 20 to 25 minutes, or until casserole is set and lightly browned. (Surface may appear slightly wet.) Let stand for 10 minutes before serving.

Nutrition Facts	Amount/serving	%DV*	Amount/serving	%DV*
Serving Size approximately ¾ cup (249g)	Total Fat 5g	7%	Total Carbohydrate 30g	11%
	Saturated Fat 3g	12%	Dietary Fiber 5g	18%
Servings per Recipe 4	Cholesterol 15mg	5%	Sugars 3g	
Calories 225 Calories from Fat 41	Sodium 285mg	12%	Protein 17g	

Vitamin A 30% • Vitamin C 53% • Calcium 23% • Iron 12%

*Percent Daily Values (DV) are based on a 2000 calorie diet.

Menu Planning Guide

One serving of this recipe provides:

1½ Vegetable
1½ Bread, Cereal, Rice & Pasta

Diet Exchanges:

1½ lean meat • 1½ starch • 1½ vegetable

Moroccan Eggplant

Serve with a soft pita loaf and fresh fruit

¾ cup ready-to-serve vegetable broth

2 teaspoons curry powder

1 teaspoon dried oregano leaves

¼ teaspoon freshly ground pepper

½ cup uncooked couscous

1 medium eggplant (1 lb.)

1 teaspoon olive oil

½ cup chopped red pepper

⅓ cup sliced fresh mushrooms

¼ cup sliced green onions (½-inch lengths)

¼ cup shredded carrot

¼ cup chopped dried dates

½ cup water

2 servings

1 Heat oven to 350°F. In 1-quart saucepan, combine broth, curry powder, oregano and ground pepper. Bring to boil over high heat. Stir in couscous. Remove from heat. Cover. Let stand for 5 minutes. Fluff couscous with fork. Set aside.

2 Cut eggplant in half lengthwise. Scoop out pulp, leaving ¼-inch shells. Coarsely chop pulp. Set shells aside.

3 Heat oil in 10-inch nonstick skillet over medium heat. Add pulp, red pepper, mushrooms, onions and carrot. Cook for 5 to 7 minutes, or until vegetables are tender, stirring frequently. Remove from heat. Stir in couscous and dates.

4 Spoon mixture evenly into shells. Arrange shells in 10-inch square casserole. Pour water into dish around shells. Partially cover dish with foil. Bake for 30 to 40 minutes, or until heated through. Serve immediately.

Nutrition Facts	Amount/serving	%DV*	Amount/serving	%DV*
Serving Size ½ eggplant (414g)	Total Fat 4g	6%	Total Carbohydrate 72g	24%
Servings per Recipe 2	Saturated Fat <1g	3%	Dietary Fiber 11g	42%
Calories 345	Cholesterol 0mg	0%	Sugars 27g	
Calories from Fat 36	Sodium 402mg	17%	Protein 9g	

Vitamin A 120% • Vitamin C 100% • Calcium 6% • Iron 15%

*Percent Daily Values (DV) are based on a 2000 calorie diet.

Menu Planning Guide

One serving of this recipe provides:

3 Vegetable
½ Fruit
2 Bread, Cereal, Rice & Pasta

Diet Exchanges:

2½ starch • 3 vegetable • 1 fruit

Veggie Lasagna

Serve with fresh honeydew and cantaloupe slices and crusty bread

12 uncooked lasagna noodles

1/3 cup dry red wine

1 medium onion, chopped (1 cup)

3 cloves garlic, minced

4 oz. fresh mushrooms, sliced (1 1/2 cups)

1 1/2 cups small broccoli flowerets

3 medium carrots, shredded (1 1/2 cups)

1/4 cup water

1 medium zucchini squash, cut into
    2 x 1/8-inch strips (1 cup)

1 medium yellow summer squash, cut into
    2 x 1/8-inch strips (1 cup)

3 cans (8 oz. each) tomato sauce

2 medium tomatoes, peeled and finely
    chopped (2 cups)

1/4 cup snipped fresh parsley

1 tablespoon dried basil leaves

1 teaspoon dried oregano leaves

1/2 teaspoon fennel seed, crushed

1/2 teaspoon pepper

1 carton (15 oz.) nonfat or low-fat ricotta
    cheese

2 cups shredded part-skim or nonfat
    mozzarella cheese

3 tablespoons shredded fresh Parmesan
    cheese (optional)

10 servings

1 Prepare noodles as directed on package. Rinse and drain. Set aside. In 12-inch non-stick skillet, heat wine over medium heat until bubbly. Add onion and garlic. Cook for 4 to 5 minutes, or until onion is tender, stirring occasionally. Stir in mushrooms, broccoli, carrots and water. Cover. Cook for 6 to 7 minutes, or until carrots are tender. Stir in squashes. Cook, uncovered, for 2 to 3 minutes, or until squashes are tender and all liquid boils off, stirring frequently. Remove from heat. Set vegetable mixture aside.

2 Heat oven to 350°F. Spray 13 x 9-inch baking dish with nonstick vegetable cooking spray. Set aside. In medium mixing bowl, combine tomato sauce, tomatoes, parsley, basil, oregano, fennel and pepper. Layer 4 noodles, half of ricotta, half of vegetable mixture, 1 1/4 cups sauce and one-third of mozzarella in prepared dish. Repeat layers once. Top with remaining 4 noodles. Spread remaining 1 1/4 cups sauce evenly over noodles.

3 Cover dish with foil. Bake for 45 to 50 minutes, or until lasagna is hot and edges are bubbly. Sprinkle remaining one-third of mozzarella and the Parmesan cheese evenly over lasagna. Bake, uncovered, for 5 to 7 minutes, or until cheese is melted. Let lasagna stand for 10 minutes before cutting.

Nutrition Facts	Amount/serving	%DV*	Amount/serving	%DV*
Serving Size 1 square (381g)	Total Fat 8g	12%	Total Carbohydrate 43g	14%
Servings per Recipe 10	Saturated Fat 4g	21%	Dietary Fiber 5g	20%
Calories 310	Cholesterol 27mg	9%	Sugars 9g	
Calories from Fat 73	Sodium 590mg	25%	Protein 18g	

Vitamin A 140% • Vitamin C 70% • Calcium 40% • Iron 20%

*Percent Daily Values (DV) are based on a 2000 calorie diet.

Menu Planning Guide

One serving of this recipe provides:
1 Milk, Yogurt & Cheese
2 Vegetable
2 Bread, Cereal, Rice & Pasta

Diet Exchanges:

1 1/2 medium-fat meat • 2 starch • 2 vegetable

Wild Rice Stuffed Squash

Serve with Creamy Baby Lima Beans (p 77) or Ricotta Polenta (p 106)

2 *small acorn squash (12 to 14 oz. each)*
½ *cup cooked wild rice*
¼ *cup dried cranberries*
¼ *cup thinly sliced mushrooms*
¼ *cup finely chopped green or red*
  cooking apple
1 *tablespoon honey*
¼ *teaspoon dried thyme leaves*
⅛ *teaspoon salt*
¼ *cup water*

4 servings

1 Heat oven to 350°F. Cut each squash in half lengthwise. Scoop out and discard seeds. Arrange halves cut-sides-up in 10-inch square casserole. Set aside.

2 Combine rice, cranberries, mushrooms, apple, honey, thyme and salt in small mixing bowl. Spoon rice mixture evenly into squash halves. Pour water into bottom of casserole. Cover.

3 Bake for 45 to 50 minutes, or until squash is tender. Let stand, covered, for 5 minutes before serving.

Nutrition Facts	Amount/serving	%DV*	Amount/serving	%DV*
Serving Size ½ squash (150g)	Total Fat <1g	0%	Total Carbohydrate 26g	9%
Servings per Recipe 4	Saturated Fat 0g	0%	Dietary Fiber 6g	22%
Calories 105	Cholesterol 0mg	0%	Sugars 9g	
Calories from Fat 3	Sodium 72mg	3%	Protein 2g	

Vitamin A 10% • Vitamin C 20% • Calcium 6% • Iron 8%
*Percent Daily Values (DV) are based on a 2000 calorie diet.

Menu Planning Guide
One serving of this recipe provides:
1 Vegetable

Diet Exchanges:
1½ starch

Cheese-stuffed Shells

Serve with a tossed green salad and crusty Italian bread

3½ oz. uncooked jumbo pasta shells (12 shells)

Filling:

1 *cup nonfat or low-fat ricotta cheese*
1 *cup shredded part-skim or nonfat*
   mozzarella cheese
½ *cup finely chopped red pepper*
½ *cup finely chopped fresh mushrooms*
½ *cup sliced green onions*
1 *clove garlic, minced*
½ *teaspoon dried oregano leaves*
¼ *teaspoon dried basil leaves*
¼ *teaspoon salt*
¼ *teaspoon pepper*

Sauce:

2 *tablespoons margarine*
2 *tablespoons all-purpose flour*
1 *clove garlic, minced*
1½ *cups skim milk*
1 *teaspoon dried oregano leaves*
½ *teaspoon dried basil leaves*
¼ *to ½ teaspoon fennel seed, crushed*

4 servings

1 Heat oven to 400°F. Prepare shells as directed on package. Rinse and drain. Set aside. In medium mixing bowl, combine filling ingredients. Stuff shells evenly with filling. Arrange shells in 8-inch square baking dish. Set aside.

2 Melt margarine in 2-quart saucepan over medium heat. Stir in flour and 1 clove garlic. Cook for 10 to 30 seconds, or until mixture bubbles, stirring constantly. Cook for additional 30 seconds, stirring constantly. Blend in remaining sauce ingredients. Cook for 5½ to 8½ minutes, or until sauce thickens and bubbles, stirring constantly.

3 Pour sauce into bottom of prepared dish. Cover dish with foil. Bake for 20 to 25 minutes, or until shells are hot and sauce bubbles.

Nutrition Facts	Amount/serving	%DV*	Amount/serving	%DV*
Serving Size 3 shells (326g)	Total Fat 12g	18%	Total Carbohydrate 44g	15%
Servings per Recipe 4	Saturated Fat 4g	22%	Dietary Fiber 4g	16%
Calories 372	Cholesterol 27mg	9%	Sugars 11g	
Calories from Fat 107	Sodium 523mg	22%	Protein 26g	

Vitamin A 60% • Vitamin C 70% • Calcium 90% • Iron 40%
*Percent Daily Values (DV) are based on a 2000 calorie diet.

Menu Planning Guide
One serving of this recipe provides:
1½ Milk, Yogurt & Cheese
 1 Vegetable
 2 Bread, Cereal, Rice & Pasta

Diet Exchanges:
2 lean meat • ½ skim milk • 2 starch
• 1 vegetable • 1 fat

Cheesy Chili Enchiladas

Serve with No-guilt Refried Beans (p 104) and Cajun Dirty Rice (p 95)

1 cup shredded nonfat or part-skim
   mozzarella cheese
1 cup finely shredded nonfat Cheddar cheese
1½ teaspoons chili powder, divided
2 cans (8 oz. each) no-salt-added tomato sauce
1 teaspoon sugar
½ teaspoon ground cumin
½ teaspoon garlic powder
¼ teaspoon cayenne
6 corn tortillas (6-inch)
1 can (4 oz.) whole green chilies, drained and
   cut into 6 strips

½ cup sliced green onions, divided
¼ cup plus 2 tablespoons chopped seeded tomato
¼ cup plus 2 tablespoons nonfat or low-fat
   sour cream

6 servings

1 Heat oven to 350°F. In small mixing bowl, combine cheeses and 1 teaspoon chili powder. Reserve ½ cup mixture. Set aside. In shallow dish, combine remaining ½ teaspoon chili powder, the tomato sauce, sugar, cumin, garlic powder and cayenne.

2 Dip both sides of 1 tortilla in sauce. Sprinkle ¼ cup cheese mixture down center of tortilla. Place 1 strip chili and 1 tablespoon onions over cheese mixture. Roll up tortilla. Place seam-side-down in 11 x 7-inch baking dish. Repeat with remaining tortillas, sauce, cheese mixture, chili strips and 5 tablespoons onions.

3 Spoon remaining sauce over enchiladas. Sprinkle with reserved cheese mixture. Cover dish with foil. Bake for 23 to 28 minutes, or until sauce is bubbly and cheese is melted. Sprinkle each serving with 1 tablespoon tomato, 1 tablespoon sour cream and 1 teaspoon remaining onions.

Nutrition Facts	Amount/serving	%DV*	Amount/serving	%DV*
Serving Size 1 enchilada (194g)	Total Fat 1g	2%	Total Carbohydrate 26g	9%
	Saturated Fat <1g	1%	Dietary Fiber 4g	16%
Servings per Recipe 6	Cholesterol 7mg	2%	Sugars 5g	
Calories 169	Sodium 365mg	15%	Protein 17g	
Calories from Fat 10	Vitamin A 25% • Vitamin C 25% • Calcium 8% • Iron 8%			
	*Percent Daily Values (DV) are based on a 2000 calorie diet.			

Menu Planning Guide
One serving of this recipe provides:
½ Milk, Yogurt & Cheese
1½ Vegetable
1 Bread, Cereal, Rice & Pasta

Diet Exchanges:
1½ lean meat • 1 starch • 1½ vegetable

Easy Leek Quiche

Serve with Hominy Sausage Succotash (p 101) or a tossed salad

1 pkg. (11 oz.) refrigerated bread stick dough
1 teaspoon olive oil
1 medium leek, thinly sliced (1½ cups)
1 clove garlic, minced
¾ cup shredded part-skim or nonfat
    mozzarella cheese
½ red pepper, cut into ¼-inch slices and
    separated into rings

1 cup evaporated skim milk
¾ cup frozen cholesterol-free egg product,
    defrosted; or 3 eggs, beaten
1½ teaspoons cornstarch
¼ teaspoon freshly ground pepper
⅛ teaspoon ground nutmeg

6 servings

1 Heat oven to 350°F. Spray 10-inch pie plate with nonstick vegetable cooking spray. Set aside. Separate and unroll individual bread sticks. On flat surface, coil strips of dough into circle. Using rolling pin, roll dough into 13-inch circle.

2 Press dough into bottom and up sides of prepared pie plate. (Dough will shrink back slightly when pressing.) Set aside. In 10-inch nonstick skillet, heat oil over medium heat. Add leek and garlic. Cook for 8 to 10 minutes, or until leek is tender and just begins to brown, stirring occasionally. Spread leek mixture in bottom of crust. Sprinkle cheese evenly over mixture.

3 Arrange pepper rings over cheese. In food processor or blender, combine remaining ingredients. Process until smooth. Pour mixture over filling. Bake for 45 to 50 minutes, or until filling is set and crust is golden brown. Let stand for 10 minutes before serving. Sprinkle with shredded fresh Parmesan cheese, if desired.

Nutrition Facts	Amount/serving	%DV*	Amount/serving	%DV*
Serving Size 1 slice (175g)	Total Fat 4g	6%	Total Carbohydrate 32g	11%
Servings per Recipe 6	Saturated Fat 1g	4%	Dietary Fiber 1g	4%
Calories 227	Cholesterol 3mg	1%	Sugars 6g	
Calories from Fat 38	Sodium 509mg	21%	Protein 15g	

Vitamin A 30% • Vitamin C 30% • Calcium 30% • Iron 15%

*Percent Daily Values (DV) are based on a 2000 calorie diet.

Menu Planning Guide
One serving of this recipe provides:
½ Milk, Yogurt & Cheese
½ Vegetable
1½ Bread, Cereal, Rice & Pasta

Diet Exchanges:
1 lean meat • ½ skim milk • 1½ starch
• ½ vegetable

Tomato Cheese Pie

Serve with Hominy Sausage Succotash (p 101)
or steamed mixed vegetables

Crust:

½ cup all-purpose flour
½ cup whole wheat flour
 1 tablespoon yellow cornmeal
¼ teaspoon salt (optional)
 3 tablespoons margarine, cut up
 3 to 4 tablespoons ice water

Filling:

 1 cup nonfat or light ricotta cheese
½ cup nonfat or low-fat cottage cheese
½ cup shredded nonfat Cheddar cheese
½ cup frozen cholesterol-free egg product,
      defrosted, or 2 eggs
 2 tablespoons all-purpose flour
½ teaspoon dried oregano leaves
¼ teaspoon garlic powder

 1 medium tomato, thinly sliced
 1 tablespoon grated Parmesan cheese (optional)
 1 tablespoon snipped fresh parsley
¼ teaspoon dried oregano leaves

6 servings

1 Heat oven to 375°F. In medium mixing bowl, combine flours, cornmeal and salt. Cut in margarine until mixture resembles coarse crumbs. Sprinkle with water, 1 table-spoon at a time, mixing with fork until particles are moistened and cling together.

2 Form dough into ball. Place between 2 sheets of wax paper. Roll out dough into 12-inch circle. Remove top sheet of wax paper. Turn circle onto 9-inch pie plate; remove second sheet of wax paper. Trim and flute edge. Set aside.

3 Combine filling ingredients in medium mixing bowl. Spoon into prepared crust. Bake for 30 minutes. Top with tomato slices. Sprinkle remaining ingredients evenly over tomato.

4 Bake for additional 10 to 15 minutes, or until knife inserted in center of pie comes out clean. Let stand for 10 minutes before serving.

Nutrition Facts	Amount/serving	%DV*	Amount/serving	%DV*
Serving Size 1 slice (129g)	Total Fat 10g	15%	Total Carbohydrate 23g	8%
Servings per Recipe 6	Saturated Fat 2g	11%	Dietary Fiber 2g	8%
Calories 231	Cholesterol 12mg	4%	Sugars 2g	
Calories from Fat 87	Sodium 350mg	15%	Protein 13g	

Vitamin A 10% • Vitamin C 8% • Calcium 30% • Iron 10%
*Percent Daily Values (DV) are based on a 2000 calorie diet.

Menu Planning Guide

One serving of this recipe provides:

½ Milk, Yogurt & Cheese
 1 Bread, Cereal, Rice & Pasta

Diet Exchanges:

1 lean meat • 1½ starch • 1 fat

Beans with Red Pepper Purée

Serve with Corn Bread Stuffed Pork Tenderloin (p 22)
or Rosemary Rainbow Trout (p 49)

1 large red pepper, seeded and cut into 1-inch
   chunks (1¹/₃ cups)
3¹/₄ cups water, divided
1 clove garlic, minced
¹/₂ teaspoon red wine vinegar
¹/₂ teaspoon salt
¹/₄ teaspoon instant chicken bouillon granules
¹/₄ teaspoon dried oregano leaves
¹/₈ teaspoon pepper
8 oz. fresh green beans
8 oz. fresh wax beans

8 servings

1 Combine red pepper, ¹/₄ cup water, the garlic, vinegar, salt, bouillon, oregano and pepper in 1-quart saucepan. Bring to boil over medium-high heat. Cover. Reduce heat to low. Simmer for 14 to 16 minutes, or until pepper is very tender. Drain. In food processor or blender, process mixture until smooth. Cover to keep warm. Set red pepper purée aside.

2 Combine beans and remaining 3 cups water in 3-quart saucepan. Bring to boil over medium-high heat. Reduce heat to low. Simmer, uncovered, for 5 minutes. Cover. Cook for 8 to 10 minutes, or until tender. Drain. Arrange beans on serving platter. Spoon purée over beans.

Microwave tip: Reduce water to 3 cups. In 1-quart casserole, combine red pepper, garlic, vinegar, salt, bouillon, oregano and pepper. Cover. Microwave at High for 8 to 11 minutes, or until pepper is very tender, stirring twice. Continue as directed.

Nutrition Facts	Amount/serving	%DV*	Amount/serving	%DV*
Serving Size approximately ¹/₂ cup (157g)	Total Fat <1g	0%	Total Carbohydrate 5g	2%
	Saturated Fat <1g	0%	Dietary Fiber 1g	5%
Servings per Recipe 8	Cholesterol 0mg	0%	Sugars 2g	
	Sodium 166mg	7%	Protein 1g	
Calories 23 Calories from Fat 2	Vitamin A 8% • Vitamin C 60% • Calcium 2% • Iron 4%			
	*Percent Daily Values (DV) are based on a 2000 calorie diet.			

Menu Planning Guide
One serving of this recipe provides:
1 Vegetable

Diet Exchanges:
1 vegetable

Carrots Gremolata

*Serve with Lime & Cumin Cornish Game Hens (p 29)
or Garlic-Herb Veal Roast (p 21)*

Gremolata*:

3   *tablespoons snipped fresh parsley*

2   *teaspoons grated lemon peel*

1   *medium clove garlic, finely minced*

4   *cups fresh whole baby carrots*

3   *cups water*

1   *teaspoon butter or margarine*

¼   *teaspoon salt*

¼   *teaspoon pepper*

8 servings

*Gremolata is a seasoning blend made of parsley, lemon peel and garlic. It is added to various dishes for a fresh, lively flavor.

1 Combine gremolata ingredients in small bowl. Cover with plastic wrap. Set aside.

2 Combine carrots and water in 3-quart saucepan. Bring to boil over high heat. Reduce heat to medium. Cover. Simmer for 8 to 10 minutes, or until carrots are tender. Drain, reserving 2 tablespoons cooking liquid.

3 Combine carrots and reserved cooking liquid in same saucepan. Add butter, salt and pepper. Cook over low heat until butter is melted, stirring frequently. Remove from heat. Stir in gremolata. Cover. Let stand for 1 minute. Serve immediately.

Nutrition Facts	Amount/serving	%DV*	Amount/serving	%DV*
Serving Size ½ cup (75g)	Total Fat 1g	1%	Total Carbohydrate 8g	3%
Servings per Recipe 8	Saturated Fat <1g	2%	Dietary Fiber 3g	10%
Calories 38	Cholesterol 1mg	0%	Sugars 3g	
Calories from Fat 5	Sodium 120mg	5%	Protein 1g	

Vitamin A 350% • Vitamin C 8% • Calcium 2% • Iron 4%

*Percent Daily Values (DV) are based on a 2000 calorie diet.

Menu Planning Guide

One serving of this recipe provides:

1 Vegetable

Diet Exchanges:

1 vegetable

Creamy Baby Lima Beans

Serve with Fillet of Sole Almondine (p 43), Wild Rice Stuffed Squash (p 63) or Roast Turkey Breast with Sweet & Sour Gravy (p 32)

2 pkgs. (9 oz. each) frozen baby lima beans
1 cup nonfat or low-fat sour cream
1 tablespoon all-purpose flour
1/2 teaspoon prepared mustard
1/4 teaspoon salt
1/8 teaspoon white pepper
1/8 teaspoon dried dill weed

8 servings

1 Prepare lima beans as directed on package. Drain. Set aside. In 2-quart saucepan, combine remaining ingredients. Stir in lima beans. Cook over low heat for 6 to 8 minutes, or until sauce is hot and flavors are blended, stirring occasionally.

Nutrition Facts	Amount/serving	%DV*	Amount/serving	%DV*
Serving Size approximately 1/2 cup (94g)	Total Fat <1g	0%	Total Carbohydrate 16g	5%
	Saturated Fat <1g	0%	Dietary Fiber 4g	16%
Servings per Recipe 8	Cholesterol 0mg	0%	Sugars 3g	
Calories 89 Calories from Fat 2	Sodium 109mg	5%	Protein 6g	

Vitamin A 2% • Vitamin C 6% • Calcium 2% • Iron 8%
*Percent Daily Values (DV) are based on a 2000 calorie diet.

Menu Planning Guide
One serving of this recipe provides:
1/2 Meat, Poultry & Fish

Diet Exchanges:
1 starch

Garlic Mashed Potatoes

Serve with Apple-Sage Stuffed Pork Loin Roast (p 11)
or Rosemary Rainbow Trout (p 49)

1½ lbs. peeled red potatoes, cut into ½-inch
   cubes (4 cups), rinsed and drained

½ cup water

2 to 4 large cloves garlic, peeled and
   quartered

⅓ cup hot skim milk (120° to 130°F)

1 tablespoon margarine

1 tablespoon dried chives

½ teaspoon salt
   Paprika (optional)

6 servings

1 Combine potatoes, water and garlic in 2-quart saucepan. Bring to boil over high heat. Cover. Reduce heat to medium-low. Simmer for 10 to 14 minutes, or until potatoes are very tender, stirring occasionally. Drain.

2 Combine potato mixture, milk, margarine, chives and salt in medium mixing bowl. Beat at medium speed of electric mixer until smooth. Before serving, sprinkle with paprika.

Microwave tip: Reduce water to ¼ cup. In 2-quart casserole, combine potatoes, water and garlic. Cover. Microwave at High for 10 to 14 minutes, or until potatoes are very tender, stirring twice. Drain. Continue as directed.

Nutrition Facts	Amount/serving	%DV*	Amount/serving	%DV*
Serving Size approximately ½ cup (120g)	Total Fat 2g	3%	Total Carbohydrate 22g	7%
	Saturated Fat <1g	2%	Dietary Fiber 2g	8%
Servings per Recipe 6	Cholesterol 0mg	0%	Sugars 2g	
Calories 112 Calories from Fat 18	Sodium 212mg	9%	Protein 2g	
	Vitamin A 2% • Vitamin C 15% • Calcium 2% • Iron 2%			
	*Percent Daily Values (DV) are based on a 2000 calorie diet.			

Menu Planning Guide

One serving of this recipe provides:

1 Vegetable

Diet Exchanges:

1½ starch

German Potato Salad

Serve with Baked Pork Schnitzel (p 15), Oven "Fried" Chicken (p 30) or Mock Fried Fish (p 46)

2 slices lean bacon, finely chopped
  (2 tablespoons)
1 lb. new potatoes, cut into quarters (3 cups)
3/4 cup water

Dressing:

3 tablespoons nonfat or low-fat mayonnaise
2 tablespoons packed brown sugar
1 tablespoon grated fresh onion with juice
1 teaspoon spicy brown mustard
3 tablespoons cider vinegar

2 tablespoons sliced green onion

6 servings

1 Cook bacon in 8-inch nonstick skillet over medium heat until crisp. Drain on paper-towel-lined plate. Set aside.

2 Combine potatoes and water in 2-quart saucepan. Bring to boil over high heat. Cover. Reduce heat to low. Simmer for 15 to 20 minutes, or until tender. Drain.

3 Combine dressing ingredients, except vinegar, in medium mixing bowl. Stir in vinegar. Add potatoes. Toss to combine. Garnish with bacon and green onion.

Nutrition Facts	Amount/serving	%DV*	Amount/serving	%DV*
Serving Size approximately 1/2 cup (102g) Servings per Recipe 6	Total Fat 1g	2%	Total Carbohydrate 22g	7%
	Saturated Fat <1g	2%	Dietary Fiber 2g	6%
	Cholesterol 2mg	0%	Sugars 6g	
Calories 104 Calories from Fat 11	Sodium 135mg	6%	Protein 2g	
	Vitamin A 0% • Vitamin C 20% • Calcium 2% • Iron 2%			
	*Percent Daily Values (DV) are based on a 2000 calorie diet.			

Menu Planning Guide

One serving of this recipe provides:

1 Vegetable

Diet Exchanges:

1½ starch

Ratatouille with Potatoes

Serve with Roasted Mediterranean Chicken (p 35)
or Roast Turkey Breast with Sweet & Sour Gravy (p 32)

2 cups water

8 oz. new potatoes, cut into ¾-inch
    cubes (1½ cups)

1 tablespoon olive oil

1 small red onion, chopped (½ cup)

2 cloves garlic, minced

1 small eggplant (10 oz.), cut into 1-inch
    chunks (4 cups)

8 oz. fresh mushrooms, sliced (3 cups)

3 Roma tomatoes, cut into 1-inch
    chunks (1½ cups)

1 medium green pepper, cut into 1-inch
    chunks (1¼ cups)

1 medium zucchini, sliced (1 cup)

½ teaspoon dried basil leaves

½ teaspoon dried thyme leaves

½ teaspoon dried oregano leaves

½ teaspoon salt

¼ teaspoon freshly ground pepper

¼ cup shredded fresh Parmesan cheese
    (optional)

6 servings

1 Place water in 8-quart stockpot. Bring to boil over high heat. Add potatoes. Return to boil. Cover. Reduce heat to medium-low. Cook for 10 to 11 minutes, or until potatoes are tender. Drain. Remove potatoes from pot. Set aside.

2 Place oil in same pot. Heat over medium heat. Add onion and garlic. Cook for 2½ to 3 minutes, or until onion is tender-crisp, stirring frequently.

3 Add remaining ingredients, except cheese. Cook for 6 to 8 minutes, or until eggplant, zucchini and tomatoes are tender, stirring frequently.

4 Add potatoes. Cook for 1 to 1½ minutes, or until hot, stirring occasionally. Sprinkle each serving evenly with cheese.

Nutrition Facts	Amount/serving	%DV*	Amount/serving	%DV*
Serving Size 1 cup (261g)	Total Fat 3g	4%	Total Carbohydrate 21g	7%
Servings per Recipe 6	Saturated Fat <1g	2%	Dietary Fiber 5g	19%
Calories 115	Cholesterol 0mg	0%	Sugars 6g	
Calories from Fat 25	Sodium 190mg	8%	Protein 4g	

Vitamin A 6% • Vitamin C 70% • Calcium 4% • Iron 10%
*Percent Daily Values (DV) are based on a 2000 calorie diet.

Menu Planning Guide
One serving of this recipe provides:
3 Vegetable

Diet Exchanges:
1 starch • 1 vegetable

Sautéed Peppers in Tarragon Vinaigrette

Serve with Fruit-stuffed Turkey Tenderloins (p 36)
or Bean Cassoulet (p 54)

Sauce:

- 2 tablespoons lemon juice
- 1 tablespoon cider vinegar
- 1 teaspoon sugar
- 1 teaspoon cornstarch
- 1 teaspoon ground cumin
- 1/2 teaspoon dried tarragon leaves
- 1/2 teaspoon salt
- 1/4 teaspoon paprika
- 1/8 teaspoon cayenne

- 2 cups red pepper cubes (1-inch cubes)
- 2 cups green pepper cubes (1-inch cubes)
- 1 teaspoon olive oil

6 servings

1 Combine sauce ingredients in 1-cup measure. Set aside. In 12-inch nonstick skillet, combine pepper cubes and oil. Cook over medium heat for 7 to 9½ minutes, or until peppers are tender-crisp, stirring frequently.

2 Stir in sauce. Cook for additional 30 to 45 seconds, or until sauce is thickened and peppers are coated, stirring constantly.

Nutrition Facts	Amount/serving	%DV*	Amount/serving	%DV*
Serving Size 1/2 cup (101g)	Total Fat 1g	2%	Total Carbohydrate 8g	3%
Servings per Recipe 6	Saturated Fat <1g	1%	Dietary Fiber 2g	8%
Calories 39	Cholesterol 0mg	0%	Sugars 4g	
Calories from Fat 9	Sodium 180mg	8%	Protein 1g	

Vitamin A 50% • Vitamin C 180% • Calcium 2% • Iron 4%
*Percent Daily Values (DV) are based on a 2000 calorie diet.

Menu Planning Guide
One serving of this recipe provides:
1 Vegetable

Diet Exchanges:
1 vegetable

Spicy Glazed Carrots

Serve with Baked Spinach Fettucini (p 53)
or Chicken & Potato Casserole (p 25)

1 *pkg. (16 oz.) frozen crinkle-cut carrots*
¼ *cup apricot preserves*
2 *tablespoons water*
¼ *teaspoon chili powder*
¼ *teaspoon salt*
⅛ *teaspoon ground ginger*
    Dash cayenne

6 servings

1 Combine all ingredients in 2-quart saucepan. Cover. Cook over medium heat for 12 to 17 minutes, or until carrots are hot, stirring occasionally.

Microwave tip: Combine all ingredients in 2-quart casserole. Cover. Microwave at High for 7 to 10 minutes, or until carrots are hot, stirring twice.

Nutrition Facts

Serving Size approximately ½ cup (80g)
Servings per Recipe 6
Calories 55
Calories from Fat 1

Amount/serving	%DV*	Amount/serving	%DV*
Total Fat <1g	0%	Total Carbohydrate 14g	5%
Saturated Fat 0g	0%	Dietary Fiber 2g	8%
Cholesterol 0mg	0%	Sugars 11g	
Sodium 132mg	6%	Protein <1g	

Vitamin A 220% • Vitamin C 4% • Calcium 2% • Iron 2%
*Percent Daily Values (DV) are based on a 2000 calorie diet.

Menu Planning Guide

One serving of this recipe provides:

1 Vegetable

Diet Exchanges:

½ starch • 1 vegetable

Spinach-stuffed Peppers

Serve with Vegetable Couscous (p 108) or Ricotta Polenta (p 106)

3 green, red or yellow peppers
8 cups water
1 pkg. (10 oz.) frozen chopped spinach
1 medium tomato, seeded and chopped (1 cup)
1 small onion, chopped (½ cup)
⅓ cup unseasoned dry bread crumbs

½ teaspoon salt
½ teaspoon pepper
¼ teaspoon garlic powder
¼ cup shredded nonfat or part-skim
     mozzarella cheese

6 servings

1 Cut each pepper in half lengthwise. Remove seeds. In 6-quart Dutch oven or stockpot, bring water to boil over high heat. Add peppers. Cook for 4 to 5 minutes, or until tender-crisp. Rinse with cold water. Drain. Arrange peppers cut-sides-up in 10-inch square casserole. Set aside.

2 Heat oven to 350°F. Prepare spinach as directed on package. Drain, pressing to remove excess moisture. In small mixing bowl, combine spinach and remaining ingredients, except cheese. Spoon spinach mixture evenly into peppers. Sprinkle cheese evenly over peppers. Bake for 25 to 30 minutes, or until cheese is melted and peppers are hot through center.

Microwave tip: Reduce water to ¼ cup. In 10-inch square casserole, arrange peppers cut-sides-up. Sprinkle with water. Cover with plastic wrap. Microwave at High for 6 to 8 minutes, or until tender-crisp, rearranging once. Drain. Continue as directed.

Nutrition Facts	Amount/serving	%DV*	Amount/serving	%DV*
Serving Size ½ pepper (118g)	Total Fat <1g	1%	Total Carbohydrate 11g	4%
	Saturated Fat <1g	1%	Dietary Fiber 2g	8%
Servings per Recipe 6	Cholesterol <1mg	0%	Sugars 3g	
Calories 60 Calories from Fat 5	Sodium 293mg	12%	Protein 4g	
	Vitamin A 60% • Vitamin C 60% • Calcium 8% • Iron 6%			
	*Percent Daily Values (DV) are based on a 2000 calorie diet.			

Menu Planning Guide

One serving of this recipe provides:
2 Vegetable

Diet Exchanges:

2 vegetable

Stuffed Onions

Serve with Ricotta Polenta (p 106) or Hominy Sausage Succotash (p 101)

4 *large white onions (8 to 9 oz. each), peeled*

Stuffing:

2 *cups dry bread cubes (1/2-inch cubes)*

1/4 *cup frozen cholesterol-free egg product, defrosted; or 1 egg, beaten*

1/4 *cup finely chopped celery*

1/4 *cup finely chopped red pepper*

2 *tablespoons snipped fresh parsley*

2 *tablespoons sesame seed, toasted*

2 *teaspoons lemon juice*

1/2 *teaspoon dried marjoram leaves*

1/4 *teaspoon pepper*

1 *cup hot water mixed with 1 teaspoon instant chicken bouillon granules*

4 servings

1 Heat oven to 375°F. Cut off tops of onions. Using serrated knife, score center of each onion.

2 Scoop out center, using grapefruit spoon, leaving 1/4-inch-thick shell. (Onion centers may be chopped and frozen for later use.) Place shells in 8-inch square baking dish. Set aside.

3 Combine stuffing ingredients in medium mixing bowl. Spoon stuffing evenly into shells. Pour bouillon over onions. Spray foil with nonstick vegetable cooking spray. Cover dish with foil. Bake for 25 to 30 minutes, or until onions are tender-crisp. Remove foil. Bake for additional 5 to 7 minutes, or until tops are light golden brown. Re-cover with foil. Let stand for 10 minutes before serving.

Nutrition Facts	Amount/serving	%DV*	Amount/serving	%DV*
Serving Size 1 onion (179g)	Total Fat 3g	4%	Total Carbohydrate 17g	6%
Servings per Recipe 4	Saturated Fat <1g	2%	Dietary Fiber 2g	8%
Calories 107	Cholesterol 0mg	0%	Sugars 5g	
Calories from Fat 25	Sodium 345mg	14%	Protein 4g	

Vitamin A 15% • Vitamin C 35% • Calcium 8% • Iron 10%

*Percent Daily Values (DV) are based on a 2000 calorie diet.

Menu Planning Guide

One serving of this recipe provides:

  1 Vegetable
1/2 Bread, Cereal, Rice & Pasta

Diet Exchanges:

1/2 starch • 1 vegetable • 1/2 fat

Tamale Pie

Serve with No-guilt Refried Beans (p 104) and Cajun Dirty Rice (p 95)

Filling:

1 can (16 oz.) whole tomatoes, drained and
    cut up
2 cups frozen corn
1 can (15 oz.) pinto beans, rinsed and drained
1 can (4 oz.) chopped green chilies
⅓ cup chopped green pepper
⅓ cup chopped onion
½ teaspoon ground cumin
½ teaspoon chili powder
¼ teaspoon dried cilantro leaves
¼ teaspoon dried oregano leaves
¼ teaspoon garlic powder

Crust:

¼ cup yellow cornmeal
½ cup all-purpose flour
1 teaspoon baking powder
1 tablespoon sugar
¼ teaspoon salt
½ cup skim milk
¼ cup frozen cholesterol-free egg product,
    defrosted, or 1 egg
1 tablespoon vegetable oil

6 servings

1 Heat oven to 350°F. In 3-quart saucepan, combine filling ingredients. Cook over medium heat for 10 to 15 minutes, or until mixture is very hot and flavors are blended, stirring occasionally. Cover to keep warm. Set aside.

2 Combine cornmeal, flour, baking powder, sugar and salt in small mixing bowl. Add remaining ingredients. Mix just until batter is blended.

3 Spoon filling into 9-inch round cake dish. Spoon batter over filling. Sprinkle top with paprika, if desired.

4 Bake for 30 to 40 minutes, or until cornmeal crust is golden brown. Let stand for 10 minutes. Garnish with red chili pepper or jalapeño pepper, if desired.

Nutrition Facts	Amount/serving	%DV*	Amount/serving	%DV*
Serving Size ⅙ pie (276g)	Total Fat 3g	5%	Total Carbohydrate 53g	18%
Servings per Recipe 6	Saturated Fat <1g	2%	Dietary Fiber 9g	37%
Calories 273	Cholesterol <1mg	0%	Sugars 8g	
Calories from Fat 29	Sodium 380mg	16%	Protein 11g	
	Vitamin A 10% • Vitamin C 35% • Calcium 15% • Iron 20%			
	*Percent Daily Values (DV) are based on a 2000 calorie diet.			

Menu Planning Guide

One serving of this recipe provides:
½ Meat, Poultry & Fish
1 Vegetable
1 Bread, Cereal, Rice & Pasta

Diet Exchanges:

3 starch • 1 vegetable

Cajun Dirty Rice

Serve with Cheesy Chili Enchiladas (p 66)
or Baked Red Snapper (p 39)

1   *stalk celery, chopped (½ cup)*

½   *cup coarsely chopped red pepper*

¼   *cup chopped onion*

1   *clove garlic, minced*

½   *teaspoon vegetable oil*

2   *cups hot water*

¾   *cup uncooked long-grain white rice,*
      rinsed and drained

1   *teaspoon instant chicken bouillon granules*

¼   *teaspoon ground cumin*

¼   *teaspoon dried thyme leaves*

¼   *teaspoon salt*

⅛   *teaspoon cayenne*

⅛   *teaspoon freshly ground pepper*

6 servings

1 Combine celery, red pepper, onion, garlic and oil in 10-inch nonstick skillet. Cook over medium heat for 5 to 6 minutes, or until celery is tender-crisp, stirring frequently. Stir in remaining ingredients. Bring to boil.

2 Cover. Reduce heat to medium-low. Simmer for 13 to 15 minutes, or until rice is tender and liquid is absorbed. Let stand, covered, for 5 minutes. Before serving, fluff rice with fork.

Nutrition Facts	Amount/serving	%DV*	Amount/serving	%DV*
Serving Size ½ cup (107g)	Total Fat 1g	1%	Total Carbohydrate 24g	8%
Servings per Recipe 6	Saturated Fat 0g	0%	Dietary Fiber 1g	4%
Calories 113	Cholesterol 0mg	0%	Sugars 1g	
Calories from Fat 6	Sodium 249mg	10%	Protein 2g	

Vitamin A 10% • Vitamin C 35% • Calcium 2% • Iron 6%
*Percent Daily Values (DV) are based on a 2000 calorie diet.

Menu Planning Guide

One serving of this recipe provides:

1 Bread, Cereal, Rice & Pasta

Diet Exchanges:

1½ starch

Dilled Barley Salad

Serve with Baked Corn Dogs (p 12) or Oven "Fried" Chicken (p 30)

3 cups water

⅔ cup uncooked medium pearled barley

½ cup nonfat or reduced-fat mayonnaise

½ cup sliced fresh mushrooms

1 medium carrot, chopped (½ cup)

½ cup red pepper strips (1 x ¼-inch strips)

⅓ cup sliced celery

2 tablespoons sliced green onion

2 teaspoons fresh lemon juice

2 teaspoons snipped fresh dill weed

¼ teaspoon salt

⅛ teaspoon freshly ground pepper

2 tablespoons finely chopped walnuts

1 tablespoon dried currants (optional)

8 servings

Tip: If desired, use 1 cup quick-cooking barley and simmer for 10 to 12 minutes.

1 Bring water to boil in 2-quart saucepan over high heat. Stir in barley. Cover. Reduce heat to low. Simmer for 45 to 50 minutes, or until barley is tender. Remove from heat. Let stand for 5 minutes. Drain. Cool completely.

2 Combine barley and remaining ingredients, except walnuts and currants, in medium salad bowl or mixing bowl. Cover with plastic wrap. Chill. Serve salad on lettuce-lined plates. Garnish servings evenly with walnuts and currants.

Nutrition Facts	Amount/serving	%DV*	Amount/serving	%DV*
Serving Size ½ cup (89g)	Total Fat 1g	2%	Total Carbohydrate 18g	6%
	Saturated Fat <1g	1%	Dietary Fiber 3g	12%
Servings per Recipe 8	Cholesterol 0mg	0%	Sugars 1g	
Calories 87	Sodium 244mg	10%	Protein 2g	
Calories from Fat 13	Vitamin A 50% • Vitamin C 25% • Calcium 2% • Iron 4%			
	*Percent Daily Values (DV) are based on a 2000 calorie diet.			

Menu Planning Guide

One serving of this recipe provides:

1 Bread, Cereal, Rice & Pasta

Diet Exchanges:

1 starch

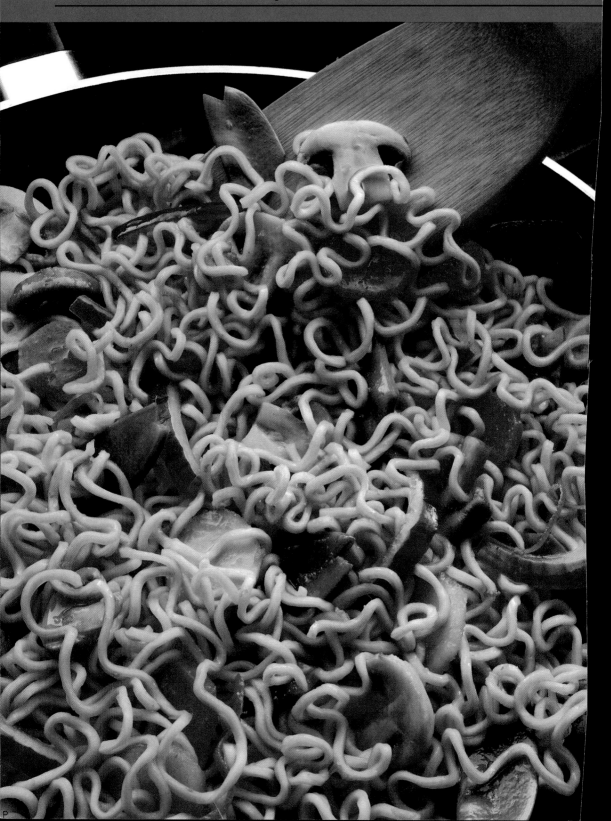

Gingered Japanese Noodles

Serve with Japanese Marinated Salmon Fillet (p 45)
or Baked Red Snapper (p 39)

uce:

cup water

tablespoons soy sauce

tablespoons rice wine vinegar

teaspoons sugar

teaspoons grated fresh gingerroot

teaspoon grated orange peel

pkg. (5 oz.) Japanese curly noodles (soba),
  coarsely broken

cup sliced fresh mushrooms

medium carrot, sliced (1/2 cup)

cup sliced halved red onion

cup sliced water chestnuts

teaspoon peanut oil

oz. fresh snow pea pods, cut into
  1-inch pieces (1 cup)

ervings

1 Combine sauce ingredients in 1-cup measure. Set aside. Prepare noodles as directed on package. Rinse and drain. Set aside.

2 Combine mushrooms, carrot, onion, water chestnuts and oil in 10-inch non-stick skillet. Cook over medium heat for 4 to 7 minutes, or until carrot is tender-crisp, stirring frequently.

3 Stir in sauce, noodles and pea pods. Cook for additional 1½ to 3 minutes, or until hot, stirring constantly.

Amount/serving	%DV*	Amount/serving	%DV*
Total Fat 1g	1%	Total Carbohydrate 17g	6%
Saturated Fat 0g	0%	Dietary Fiber 2g	8%
Cholesterol 0mg	0%	Sugars 3g	
Sodium 294mg	12%	Protein 4g	

utrition acts

ving Size
cup (116g)
vings
er Recipe 8
ories 83
alories
om Fat 6

Vitamin A 40% • Vitamin C 20% • Calcium 2% • Iron 4%
*Percent Daily Values (DV) are based on a 2000 calorie diet.

Menu Planning Guide
One serving of this recipe provides:
1 Bread, Cereal, Rice & Pasta

Diet Exchanges:
1 starch

Hominy Sausage Succotash

*Serve with Easy Leek Quiche (p 69), Tomato Cheese Pie (p 71)
or Oven "Fried" Chicken (p 30)*

1 teaspoon vegetable oil

2 cup chopped red pepper

1 can (15½ oz.) white hominy, rinsed and
    drained

1 pkg. (10 oz.) frozen baby lima beans

4 oz. low-fat smoked Kielbasa sausage,
    coarsely chopped and browned*

4 cup water

2 teaspoons paprika

2 teaspoon pepper

1 tablespoon snipped fresh parsley (optional)

ervings

brown sausage, cook it in a nonstick skillet
r medium heat, stirring occasionally.

1 Heat oil in 3-quart saucepan over medium-high heat. Add chopped pepper. Cook for 1 to 1½ minutes, or until tender-crisp, stirring frequently.

2 Stir in remaining ingredients, except parsley. Cook for 7 to 9 minutes, or until succotash is hot and liquid is slightly reduced, stirring occasionally. Remove from heat. Stir in parsley.

Nutrition Facts	Amount/serving	%DV*	Amount/serving	%DV*
	Total Fat 2g	3%	Total Carbohydrate 19g	6%
erving Size approximately ½ cup (130g) ervings per Recipe 8	Saturated Fat <1g	2%	Dietary Fiber 6g	23%
	Cholesterol 6mg	2%	Sugars 2g	
alories 106 Calories from Fat 15	Sodium 233mg	10%	Protein 6g	

Vitamin A 15% • Vitamin C 30% • Calcium 2% • Iron 8%
*Percent Daily Values (DV) are based on a 2000 calorie diet.

Menu Planning Guide
One serving of this recipe provides:
1 Vegetable

Diet Exchanges:
½ lean meat • 1 starch

Mushroom & Lemon Penne

Serve with Rosemary Rainbow Trout (p 49)
or Roasted Mediterranean Chicken (p 35)

8 oz. uncooked penne pasta (about 3 cups)

2 teaspoons olive oil, divided

8 oz. fresh mushrooms, thickly sliced (3 cups)

1 clove garlic, minced

1 teaspoon grated lemon peel

1 tablespoon fresh lemon juice

1 tablespoon snipped fresh parsley

1/2 teaspoon salt

1/8 teaspoon freshly ground pepper

1/8 teaspoon cayenne

8 servings

1 Prepare pasta as directed on package until *al dente*. Meanwhile, in 10-inch nonstick skillet, heat 1 teaspoon oil over medium-high heat. Add mushrooms and garlic. Cook for 8 to 12 minutes, or until mushrooms are lightly browned, stirring frequently. Remove from heat.

2 Drain pasta. In large mixing bowl or serving bowl, combine pasta, mushrooms, remaining 1 teaspoon oil and remaining ingredients. Toss to combine. Serve immediately.

Nutrition Facts	Amount/serving	%DV*	Amount/serving	%DV*
Serving Size 1/2 cup (122g)	Total Fat 2g	3%	Total Carbohydrate 24g	8%
Servings per Recipe 8	Saturated Fat <1g	2%	Dietary Fiber 2g	8%
Calories 131	Cholesterol 0mg	0%	Sugars 1g	
Calories from Fat 17	Sodium 135mg	6%	Protein 5g	

Vitamin A 0% • Vitamin C 6% • Calcium 0% • Iron 10%
*Percent Daily Values (DV) are based on a 2000 calorie diet.

Menu Planning Guide
One serving of this recipe provides:
1/2 Vegetable
1 Bread, Cereal, Rice & Pasta

Diet Exchanges:
1 1/2 starch • 1/2 vegetable

No-guilt Refried Beans

Serve with Cheesy Chili Enchiladas (p 66) or Tamale Pie (p 92)

1 can (16 oz.) pinto beans, rinsed and
    drained
¼ cup thick and chunky salsa
2 tablespoons finely chopped onion
⅛ teaspoon garlic powder
1 tablespoon margarine

4 servings

1 Combine beans, salsa, onion and garlic powder in 2-quart saucepan. Bring mixture to boil over medium-high heat, stirring occasionally. Reduce heat to medium-low. Simmer for 7 to 10 minutes, or until onion is translucent, stirring occasionally.

2 Add margarine. Stir until melted. In food processor or blender, process mixture until smooth. Serve as a taco ingredient or chip and vegetable dip.

Nutrition Facts	Amount/serving	%DV*	Amount/serving	%DV*
Serving Size approximately ¼ cup (121g)	Total Fat 3g	5%	Total Carbohydrate 26g	9%
	Saturated Fat <1g	4%	Dietary Fiber 9g	36%
Servings per Recipe 4	Cholesterol 0mg	0%	Sugars 3g	
Calories 165	Sodium 94mg	4%	Protein 8g	
Calories from Fat 31	Vitamin A 8% • Vitamin C 15% • Calcium 6% • Iron 15%			
	*Percent Daily Values (DV) are based on a 2000 calorie diet.			

Menu Planning Guide
One serving of this recipe provides:
½ Meat, Poultry & Fish

Diet Exchanges:
2 starch

Ricotta Polenta

Serve with Spinach Meatloaf with Fresh Tomato Sauce (p 18),
Spinach-stuffed Peppers (p 89) or Wild Rice Stuffed Squash (p 63)

1   cup water
¾   cup yellow cornmeal
¼   cup snipped fresh parsley
¼   teaspoon salt
¼   teaspoon cayenne
1   can (12 oz.) evaporated skim milk
½   cup nonfat or low-fat ricotta cheese
¼   cup shredded fresh Parmesan cheese

6 servings

Variation: Spray 9-inch round baking dish with nonstick vegetable cooking spray. Set aside. Prepare polenta as directed, except immediately spread polenta evenly in prepared dish. Loosely cover with plastic wrap. Refrigerate until set. To serve, cut into wedges. Microwave individual wedges for 1 to 1½ minutes, or until hot, rotating plate once. (Or, place under broiler with surface of polenta 4 to 5 inches from heat. Broil for 5 to 7 minutes, or until hot.) Sprinkle with additional shredded fresh Parmesan cheese and serve with hot low-fat pasta sauce, if desired.

1 Combine water, cornmeal, parsley, salt and cayenne in small mixing bowl. Let stand for 10 minutes. Set aside.

2 Bring milk to simmer in 2-quart saucepan over medium heat. Stir in cornmeal mixture. Cook for 5 to 7 minutes, or until desired thickness, stirring constantly. Remove from heat.

3 Stir in cheeses. Serve immediately. Sprinkle each serving with additional shredded fresh Parmesan cheese, if desired

Nutrition Facts	Amount/serving	%DV*	Amount/serving	%DV*
Serving Size ½ cup (141g)	Total Fat 2g	2%	Total Carbohydrate 21g	7%
	Saturated Fat 1g	5%	Dietary Fiber 1g	4%
Servings per Recipe 6	Cholesterol 9mg	3%	Sugars 7g	
Calories 142	Sodium 275mg	11%	Protein 11g	
Calories from Fat 15	Vitamin A 10% • Vitamin C 6% • Calcium 35% • Iron 6%			
	*Percent Daily Values (DV) are based on a 2000 calorie diet.			

Menu Planning Guide

One serving of this recipe provides:
1 Milk, Yogurt & Cheese
1 Bread, Cereal, Rice & Pasta

Diet Exchanges:

½ lean meat • ½ skim milk • 1 starch

Vegetable Couscous

Serve with Spinach-stuffed Peppers (p 89)
or Fillet of Sole Almondine (p 43)

1 cup ready-to-serve chicken broth
⅔ cup uncooked couscous
1½ teaspoons vegetable oil, divided
1 medium carrot, peeled lengthwise
     into strips
½ cup sliced halved red onion
½ cup red or green pepper chunks (½-inch
     chunks)
1 stalk celery, sliced (½ cup)
2 tablespoons snipped fresh basil leaves

8 servings

1 Bring broth to boil in 1-quart saucepan over medium-high heat. Stir in couscous. Cover. Remove from heat. Let stand for 5 minutes. Fluff couscous lightly with fork. Add ½ teaspoon oil, stirring to coat. Cover to keep warm. Set aside.

2 Heat remaining 1 teaspoon oil in wok over high heat. Add carrot, onion, pepper and celery. Cook for 2½ to 3 minutes, or until vegetables are tender-crisp, stirring constantly. Gently stir in couscous and basil. Cook for 1 to 2 minutes, or just until hot, stirring constantly. Remove from heat. Serve immediately.

Nutrition Facts	Amount/serving	%DV*	Amount/serving	%DV*
Serving Size ½ cup (74g)	Total Fat 1g	2%	Total Carbohydrate 11g	4%
	Saturated Fat <1g	1%	Dietary Fiber 1g	5%
Servings per Recipe 8	Cholesterol 0mg	0%	Sugars 2g	
Calories 66	Sodium 110mg	5%	Protein 2g	
Calories from Fat 11	Vitamin A 60% • Vitamin C 25% • Calcium 2% • Iron 2%			
	*Percent Daily Values (DV) are based on a 2000 calorie diet.			

Menu Planning Guide
One serving of this recipe provides:
½ Vegetable
½ Bread, Cereal, Rice & Pasta

Diet Exchanges:
½ starch • ½ vegetable

Index

Cy DeCosse Incorporated offers
a variety of how-to books.
For information write:
    Cy DeCosse Subscriber Books
    5900 Green Oak Drive
    Minnetonka, MN 55343